2

W9-BVQ-095

A12901 740643

3/08

# The Stock Market

# The Stock Market

## RIK W. HAFER AND SCOTT E. HEIN

GREENWOOD GUIDES TO BUSINESS AND ECONOMICS
Wesley B. Truitt, Series Editor

GREENWOOD PRESS
WESTPORT, CONNECTICUT • LONDON

HG
4551
.H23
2007

**Library of Congress Cataloging-in-Publication Data**

Hafer, R. W. (Rik W.)
　The stock market / Rik W. Hafer and Scott E. Hein.
　　p. cm. — (Greenwood guides to business and economics,
ISSN 1559–2367)
　Includes bibliographical references and index.
　ISBN 0–313–33824–8 (alk. paper)
　1. Stock exchanges.　2. Stock exchanges—United States.　I. Hein,
Scott E., 1949–　II. Title.
　HG4551.H23 2007
　332.64'2—dc22　　　　2006029484

British Library Cataloguing-in-Publication Data is available.

Library of Congress Catalog Card Number: 2006029484
ISBN: 0–313–33824–8
ISSN: 1559–2367

First published in 2007

Greenwood Press, 88 Post Road West, Westport, CT 06881
An imprint of Greenwood Publishing Group, Inc.
www.greenwood.com

Printed in the United States of America

The paper used in this book complies with the
Permanent Paper Standard issued by the National
Information Standards Organization (Z39.48–1984).

10　9　8　7　6　5　4　3　2　1

To
Gail and Cait
Ellen, Tracey, and Jocelyn

# Contents

# Illustrations

# Series Foreword

Scanning the pages of the newspaper on any given day, you'll find headlines like these:

"OPEC Points to Supply Chains as Cause of Price Hikes"

"Business Groups Warn of Danger of Takeover Proposals"

"U.S. Durable Goods Orders Jump 3.3%"

"Dollar Hits Two-Year High Versus Yen"

"Credibility of WTO at Stake in Trade Talks"

"U.S. GDP Growth Slows While Fed Fears Inflation Growth"

If this seems like gibberish to you, then you are in good company. To most people, the language of economics is mysterious, intimidating, impenetrable. But with economic forces profoundly influencing our daily lives, being familiar with the ideas and principles of business and economics is vital to our welfare. From fluctuating interest rates to rising gasoline prices to corporate misconduct to the vicissitudes of the stock market to the rippling effects of protests and strikes overseas or natural disasters closer to home, "the economy" is not an abstraction. As Robert Duvall, president and CEO of the National Council on Economic Education, has forcefully argued, "Young people in our country need to know that economic education is not an option. Economic literacy is a vital skill, just as vital as reading literacy."[1] Understanding economics is a skill that will help you interpret current events that are playing out on a global scale, or in your checkbook, ultimately helping you make wiser choices about how you manage your financial resources—today and tomorrow.

It is the goal of this series, Greenwood Guides to Business and Economics, to promote economic literacy and improve economic decision-making. All seven books in the series are written for the general reader, high school and college student, or the business manager, entrepreneur, or graduate student in business and economics looking for a handy refresher. They have been written by experts in their respective fields for nonexpert readers. The approach throughout is at a "basic" level to maximize understanding and demystify how our business-driven economy really works.

Each book in the series is an essential guide to the topic of that volume, providing an introduction to its respective subject area. The series as a whole constitutes a library of information, up-to-date data, definitions of terms, and resources, covering all aspects of economic activity. Volumes feature such elements as timelines, glossaries, and examples and illustrations that bring the concepts to life and present them in a historical and cultural context.

The selection of the seven titles and their authors has been the work of an Editorial Advisory Board, whose members are the following: Alan Carsrud, Florida International University; Alan Reynolds, Cato Institute; Robert Spich, University of California, Los Angeles; Wesley Truitt, Loyola Marymount University; Walter E. Williams, George Mason University; and Charles Wolf, Jr., RAND Corporation.

As series editor, I served as chairman of the Editorial Advisory Board and want to express my appreciation to each of these distinguished individuals for their dedicated service in helping to bring this important series to reality.

The seven volumes in the series are as follows:

*The Corporation* by Wesley B. Truitt, Loyola Marymount University

*Entrepreneurship* by Alan L. Carsrud, Florida International University, and Malin Brännback, Åbo Akademi University

*Globalization* by Robert Spich, Christopher Thornberg, and Jeany Zhao, UCLA

*Income and Wealth* by Alan Reynolds, Cato Institute

*Money* by Mark F. Dobeck and Euel Elliott, University of Texas at Dallas

*The National Economy* by Bradley A. Hansen, University of Mary Washington

*The Stock Market* by Rik W. Hafer, Southern Illinois University–Edwardsville, and Scott E. Hein, Texas Tech University

Special thanks to our senior editor at Greenwood, Nick Philipson, for conceiving the idea of the series and for sponsoring it within Greenwood Press.

The overriding purpose of each of these books and the series as a whole is, as Walter Williams so aptly put it, to "push back the frontiers of ignorance."

Wesley B. Truitt, Series Editor

## NOTE

1. Quoted in Gary H. Stern, "Do We Know Enough about Economics?" *The Region*, Federal Reserve Bank of Minneapolis (December 1998).

# Preface and Acknowledgments

Readers familiar with the complexities of the stock market may be struck by the brevity of this book. Our goal is not to cover the entire landscape encompassing the stock market and its related areas. What the book does accomplish is to give you a glimpse into the many-faceted subject of stocks and financial markets. With this in mind, the treatment is not exhaustive but, we trust, inclusive enough to provide an overview of the stock market: how it began, how it functions, and some of the instruments traded, from common to arcane. Although the focus is primarily on the U.S. stock market, given the increasingly interrelated nature of financial markets, there is some discussion of the development of foreign stock exchanges and how their formation may be related to economic development.

Today's stock market, both here and abroad, represents the culmination of a long development in financial assets and the procedures by which they are traded. While early markets traded shares of stocks in companies, something that continues to this day, modern stock exchanges allow for the trading of many more sophisticated assets. Options, other derivatives, and the like are all part of the market's offering. And as the sophistication of assets traded has increased, so have the methods by which they are traded. From the early days when the introduction of the telegraph and telephone connected investors across the country with the exchanges, modern technology in the form of electronic trading, such as the National Association of Securities Dealers Automated Quotation (NASDAQ) exchange, is predictably crowding out the quaint, though antiquated, face-to-face kind of trading. And such technology means more efficient and speedy flows of information. Consequently, modern traders can watch, in real time, the value of their stocks change on their laptop computers.

Such flow of information creates problems for regulating the market. Regulations passed in past decades are made obsolete by new technologies and new products. The age-old debate whether regulation helps or hinders markets allocate financial capital continues, but there is some evidence that unbridled trading can lead to undesirable consequences. For many, the stock market crashes of 1929, 1987, and the meltdown that began in 2000 are evidence that some regulation may be optimal. Without trying to solve the debate, the notion of why stock markets are regulated and how key regulations developed are covered.

In trying to cover the topic, it is necessary to use a language that may seem arcane. Like any other topic, there are terms specific to finance and economics and stock markets. Such language will creep into the discussion, hopefully only when necessary. At all times, however, the goal is to present the material in a manner that is accessible to the general reader. If we are successful, this book will not be the last book on the topic you pick up.

A number of people helped us bring this book into existence. We would like to thank Nick Philipson, Senior editor for Business/Economics at Greenwood Publishing Group, and Wesley Truitt, editor of this series, for involving us with this project and providing encouragement, comments, and assistance along the way. We also thank David Amable for his help in searching out data and Stephanie Leskovisek, Janet Novosad, and Shelby Otta for getting our rough drafts into more readable form. Tracey Griffith read and commented on much of the book in earlier drafts and she expertly compiled the glossary that accompanies the book. For this, we owe her a special debt of gratitude. We also would like to acknowledge the benefits we have gained from many teachers and colleagues, too many to name individually, who helped in our understanding of the stock market. Finally, we especially thank our wives Gail and Ellen and all of our children, first for their inspiration, and second for their forbearance through the project. We hope that they approve of the results.

# Chronology

**1682**    Exchange Rules and Regulation enacted in Frankfurt, Germany, officially establishing the stock exchange.

**1790**    Federal government refinances Revolutionary War debt. This includes both federal and state debt, totaling almost $80 million in bonds. The first significant issue of publicly traded securities.

**1792**    The Buttonwood Agreement is signed on May 17 marking the beginning of the organized securities trading in what would become the New York Stock Exchange (NYSE). The Bank of New York is the first company listed.

**1801**    After a century of unregulated trading, the London Stock Exchange is officially created.

**1817**    The New York Stock & Exchange Board (NYS&EB) is created and locates at 40 Wall Street.

**1835**    A fire destroys over 700 buildings in lower Manhattan forcing the NYS&EB to relocate to temporary headquarters.

**1844**    The invention and use of the telegraph allows brokers and investors outside of New York City to communicate with the stock exchange.

**1851**    Amsterdam Stock Exchange Association forms to regulate share trading in the Amsterdam exchange, one of the world's oldest.

**1857**        A major financial panic hits Wall Street with the collapse of the Ohio Insurance & Trust Company.

**1861**        With the outbreak of the Civil War in April, the NYS&EB suspends trading in Southern state bonds.

**1863**        The board adopts the name New York Stock Exchange.

**1865**        The NYSE moves to new headquarters on Broad Street. Wall and Broad Streets becomes a hub of securities trading. In that same year, the exchange closes for more than a week following the assassination of President Lincoln.

**1866**        The completion of the trans-Atlantic cable allows traders in New York and London securities markets to communicate in hours, not weeks.

**1867**        The stock ticker, invented by Edward A. Calahan, is introduced. The ticker provides investors outside of New York with current prices on the exchange.

**1869**        Goldman founded by Marcus Goldman. Samuel Sachs, his son-in-law, becomes senior partner in 1904 leading to the firm's name change to Goldman Sachs.

**1870**        Jay Gould and his associates fail to corner the gold market through speculative manipulation. The result is a dramatic fall in gold prices and hundreds of business failures. A significant break occurs in the stock market on September 24, referred to as Black Friday.

**1871**        NYSE adopts the practice of continuous trading, thus replacing the call market approach used since the early 1800s. Brokers dealing in certain stocks must remain in one location on the trading floor thus giving rise to specialists.

**1873**        The Philadelphia banking firm of Jay Cooke & Company fails due to huge losses in speculative trading in railroad stocks. The NYSE closes for ten days due to the ensuing financial panic.

**1878**        The first telephone is installed on the trading floor of the NYSE.

                Stock Exchange Ordinance enacted and Tokyo Stock Exchange Co., Ltd. is established.

1886     Trading on the NYSE hits 1 million shares for the first time on December 15.

1893     Panic of 1893, one of the most severe economic downturns in U.S. economic history, causes widespread financial distress. Stock market losses are large.

1896     The *Wall Street Journal* publishes the Dow Jones Industrial Average (DJIA) for the first time. The index is comprised of twelve stocks and has an initial value of 40.74.

1903     On April 22 the NYSE moves to its present site. The trading floor has been in use since that time.

1907     Initiated by the financial troubles of the Knickerbocker Trust, a leading New York banking firm, stock prices tumble. The panic of 1907 ensues. Financier J. P. Morgan mobilizes a bailout of banks that stems the decline in stock prices.

1910     Arthur, Herbert, and Percy Salomon form Salomon Bros. & Company.

1913     President Wilson signs the Federal Reserve Act in December, creating the Federal Reserve System.

1914     Due to events in World War I, rapidly declining share prices prompts the NYSE to close on July 31. The exchange does not open until mid-December, the longest period of time that the exchange has not operated.

1915     Beginning in 1915 share market prices are quoted in dollars, not as a percent of their par value.

            Charles E. Merrill & Co. becomes Merrill, Lynch & Co.

1920     The NYSE creates the Stock Clearing Corporation, a centralized system that speeds up the delivery and clearing of securities among exchange members, banks, and trust companies.

1924     Massachusetts Investors Trust is founded, the first open-end mutual fund in the United States.

1927     First American Depository Receipt (ADR) is created by J. P. Morgan. The purpose is to facilitate trading by U.S. investors in the British firm Selfridge.

1929     Share prices fall sharply on Black Thursday, October 24, 1929. Over 13 million shares traded that day, a record up to that time. On October 29, Black Tuesday, a record 16 million shares are traded and the DJIA falls more than 11 percent. The DJIA hit bottom in July 1932, nearly 90 percent below its September 1929 peak.

**1929–1933**   The Great Depression.

**1933**   The NYSE closes on March 4 when President Franklin Roosevelt declares a bank holiday. The holiday, a time when banks would cease operations, often marks the end of the Great Depression.

Congress passes the Banking Act of 1933. The act separates commercial and investment banking, and creates the Federal Deposit Insurance Corporation (FDIC).

Congress passes the Securities Act of 1933. Called the "truth in securities" act, it requires companies to provide investors with more information about company business and financial information.

**1934**   Congress passes the Securities Exchange Act of 1934. The act requires increased disclosure by firms to investors to thwart speculative trading and fraud that occurred prior to the 1929 market crash. The Securities and Exchange Commission (SEC) is created as part of the Act.

**1935**   Harold Stanley and Henry S. Morgan, together with other employees from J. P. Morgan & Co. and Drexel & Co., form the investment banking firm of Morgan Stanley & Co. In 1941 the firm joins the NYSE and enters the brokerage business.

**1938**   William McChesney Martin, Jr. becomes the first full-time, salaried president of the NYSE. Martin, who later would serve as chairman of the Federal Reserve Board of Governors, reorganizes the exchange.

Charles D. Barney & Co. merges with Edward B. Smith & Co. to form Smith Barney & Co.

**1940**   Investment Advisors Act is passed. It requires financial advisors to register with the SEC.

**1941**   The constitution of the NYSE is revised to centralize authority over the exchange's operations in the office of the president.

1943 Women are allowed to work on the trading floor for the first time in NYSE history.

1945 The NYSE closes on August 15 and 16 to celebrate V-J Day, the end of World War II.

   Frankfurt Exchange reopens in September after being closed for six months.

1949 In April the Tokyo Stock Exchange reopens in its modern form.

1950 The Nikkei 225 is first reported by the Tokyo Stock Exchange.

1953 Although it began as an outdoor market on Broad Street in the 1800s, it is not until 1953 that the American Stock Exchange (AMEX) is so named.

1954 The NYSE launches its Monthly Investment Plan (MIP) allowing individuals to make a minimum monthly investment of only $40 through special accounts with NYSE member firms.

1955 Chase Manhattan Bank formed when Bank of the Manhattan Company (est. 1799) purchases Chase National Bank (est. 1877).

1957 S&P 500 introduced by Standard and Poor's. The original index includes 233 firms, expanded to 500 in 1957.

1958 Legislation creating the S Corporation passed and signed into law.

1961 Trading on the NYSE exceeds 4 million shares.

1962 Kmart, Target, and Wal-Mart begin operations. Wal-Mart would grow to become the nation's largest retailer.

1963 The assassination of President John Kennedy prompts the NYSE to close early to avoid panic selling.

1964 The 900 ticker replaces the black box ticker, doubling the speed at which price information flows.

1966 The NYSE Composite Index is established, including all listed common stocks. The initial value of the index is fifty. Also, the first electronic ticker displays are introduced.

**1967**      Muriel Siebert becomes the first woman member of the NYSE.

**1968**      Intel is founded by Gordon E. Moore and Robert Noyce. Intel grows to become the world's largest semiconductor company.

**1969**      Tokyo Stock Price Index (TOPIX) is introduced.

The Hang Seng Index is introduced in the Hong Kong Stock Exchange.

**1970**      Joseph L. Searles III becomes the NYSE's first black member.

Securities Investors Protection Act is passed. The act creates the Securities Protection Corporation (SIPC), an insurance company to stock investors. The SIPC protects investors from losses due to broker malfeasance and fraud.

**1971**      The NYSE becomes the New York Stock Exchange, Inc. following incorporation as a not-for-profit corporation in February.

The National Association of Securities Dealers Automated Quotations (NASDAQ) is formed. It is the world's first totally electronic stock exchange in the world.

**1972**      The DJIA passes through the 1,000 level on November 14, 1972, reaching 1,003.16 at the close of trading.

**1973**      The Depository Trust Company is established to serve as a central depository for securities certificates based on electronically recording stock ownership transfers.

Drexel & Co. merges with Burnham & Co. to form Drexel Burnham, one of the most successful investment banks in the 1970s and 1980s. The company files for bankruptcy in 1990 after the scandals rock the firm and lead to the indictments of David Levine and Michael Milken.

Chicago Board Options Exchange (CBOE) opens, the world's first stock options exchange.

First female members admitted to the London Stock Exchange.

**1975**      Charles Schwab opens the discount brokerage firm. Charles Schwab is acquired by Bank of America in 1983.

Microsoft founded in Albuquerque, NM, by Bill Gates and
Paul Allen.

1976     The Designated Order Turnaround (DOT) system is introduced to facilitate the trading of smaller orders. In May
specialists begin trading in lots of less than 100 shares, the so-
called odd lot trades.

The first retail fund index is created: First Index Investment
Trust (now called Vanguard 500 Index).

Apple Computer is formed in April by creators of the Apple I
personal computer, Steve Jobs and Steve Wozniak.

1977     Chicago Board of Trade (CBOT) offers first U.S. Treasury
Bond futures contract.

The TSE 300 Composite Index is introduced by the Toronto
Stock Exchange. This same year, the Toronto exchange
introduces its Computer Assisted Trading System (CATS).

1978     The Integrated Trading System (ITS) begins operation. The
ITS electronically links the NYSE and other exchanges to
permit fuller access by brokers to security prices nationwide.

1979     The New York Futures Exchange (NYFE) is formed by the
NYSE.

1981     Congress creates the Individual Retirement Account (IRA).

1982     Shares traded on the NYSE exceed 100 million for the first
time.

1984     To handle increased trading pressure, the Super Dot 250 is
inaugurated. The Super Dot 250 links member firms to
specialist posts and represents yet another advance in electronic trading.

FTSE 100, representing the 100 largest firms traded on the
London Stock Exchange, is introduced. FTSE is a mnemonic
for Financial Times Stock Exchange.

1985     Trading hours are changed to their current times of 9:30 A.M.
to 4:00 P.M., Eastern. In March Ronald Reagan becomes the
first sitting U.S. president to visit the NYSE trading floor.

1986     Deregulation of the London stock trading begins, known as
the Big Bang.

**1987**      The DJIA experiences its largest one-day percentage drop on October 19. The DJIA fell 508 points, or 22.61 percent on that day with trading volume surging to a record 604 million shares. This trading volume was exceeded the very next day with over 608 million shares traded.

President Reagan creates the Presidential Task Force on Market Mechanisms, headed by Treasury Secretary Brady. The task force proposes "circuit breakers" to halt trading when price declines become too large.

**1988**      To prevent future occurrences of wide price swings as in October 1987, the SEC approves circuit breakers. Circuit breakers halt trading when share prices become too volatile.

**1989**      Michael Milken, known as the "king of junk bonds," is indicted on ninety-eight counts of racketeering and fraud. He eventually serves twenty-two months in jail (March 1991 through January 1993) and pays a fine in the millions.

**1991**      The DJIA closes above 3,000 for the first time on April 17. Off-hours trading sessions are begun by the NYSE.

**1992**      The NYSE celebrates its bicentennial on May 17. Former president Ronald Reagan and former Soviet president Mikhail Gorbachev tour the trading floor.

**1993**      The Integrated Technology Plan is introduced to improve the capacity and efficiency of trading floor operations. The NYSE now trades over 1 billion shares daily.

**1994**      The uniform shareholders' voting rights policy is adopted by the NYSE, the AMEX, and the National Associations of Securities Dealers.

**1995**      Improvements occur in the use of cellular technology, flat screen monitors, fiber optics, and hand-held terminals. The DJIA passes through 5,000, closing at 5,023.55 on November 21.

Barrings Bank, one of the oldest merchant banks in England, collapses due to speculative trading losses by one of its traders, Nick Leeson.

eBay is founded in San Jose, CA, by Pierre Omidyar as Auctionweb. The name is changed in 1997 and it goes public in September 1998.

**1996**
Real-time quotes are listed on CNBC and CNN-FN. Prior to this all quotes were delayed twenty minutes. This year saw a continuation of a trend: the listing of non-U.S. companies. In July the number reached 290 companies with a volume of over 681 million shares traded.

The Toronto Stock Exchange introduces decimal trading.

Alan Greenspan, the chairman of the Board of Governors of the Federal Reserve System, coins the phrase "irrational exuberance" in a speech to the American Enterprise Institute in Washington, D.C.

**1997**
The Wireless Data System is introduced to allow brokers to receive orders and execute sales from any location on the floor.

Asian Crisis hits as speculative trading drives down the exchange value of the Thai baht. The financial crisis spreads to other major Asian currencies and financial markets.

On October 27 the DJIA drops 514 points triggering the circuit breaker rule for the first time. Trading in stocks is halted at 3:30 P.M. The following day trading volume exceeds 1.2 billion shares as the DJIA rebounds 337.17 points.

The Toronto Exchange moves to electronic, floorless trading, one of the world's first exchanges to do so.

**1998**
In April, volatility in the market leads the NYSE to invoke new circuit breaker rules when the DJIA declined 10, 20, and 30 percent.

Russian financial system collapses in August following default by Russian government. DJIA drops 512 points (6.4 percent) on August 31.

Long-Term Capital Management (LTCM), a major hedge firm, narrowly escapes collapse due to events surrounding financial problems in Russia. LTCM is bailed out by a consortium of banks through a deal brokered by the New York Federal Reserve.

Google incorporates.

The AMEX and NASDAQ merge.

**1999**    March 19 marks the first time the DJIA closes above 10,000. Since 1991 the DJIA has increased more than three-fold.

AOL acquires Time Warner in one of the largest takeovers to date.

Barbara G. Stymiest is appointed as the president and CEO of the Toronto Stock Exchange. She becomes the first woman to head a major North American stock exchange.

**2000**    The feared "millennium bug" fails to materialize.

The DJIA reaches its all-time high of 11,722.98 on January 14. On March 16 the DJIA experiences the largest single-day increase of 499.19 points. A month later, on April 14, the DJIA experiences its single-largest one-day point decline, falling 617.78 points. The bull market of the 1990s is over.

J. P. Morgan Chase & Co. formed when Chemical Bank (est. 1823) and J. P. Morgan & Co. (est. 1895) merge.

Stock Exchange of Hong Kong and Hong Kong Securities Clearing Co. merge to form Hong Kong Exchanges & Clearing, Ltd., better known as HEKx.

The stock exchanges of Amsterdam, Brussels, and Paris merge to form Euronext N.V., the first cross-border exchange in Europe.

**2001**    Volume of trading on the NYSE exceeded 2 billion shares for the first time on January 4.

Decimal pricing of all NYSE stocks is fully implemented on January 29.

The Enron Corporation files for bankruptcy.

On September 11, terrorist attacks destroy the World Trade Center. The NYSE closes for four days—its longest closure since 1933—and reopens on September 17 with a record trading volume of 2.37 billion shares.

**2002**    The Sarbanes-Oxley Act, which aims to improve the accuracy and reliability of firm data through increased corporate disclosures, goes into effect.

Chicago Mercantile Exchange (CME) becomes the first publicly traded U.S. financial exchange when its shares are traded on the NYSE.

Arthur Andersen, LLP, the Chicago-based accounting firm, is convicted of obstruction of justice in its role as auditor of Enron.

**2003**     As a fallout of recent corporate scandals, the SEC approves the NYSE's new corporate governance standards for listed companies. This requires boards of NYSE-listed companies to have a majority of independent directors, and requires that nomination, compensation, and audit committee consist solely of independent directors.

**2004**     J. P. Morgan Chase & Co. merges with Bank One to form one of the nation's largest financial services companies.

Google goes public on August 19, 2004.

**2005**     The NYSE and ArcaEx announce on April 20 that they have entered a definitive merger agreement leading to the combined entity, NYSE Group, Inc., becoming a publicly-held company. June 24 sees the NYSE handle its largest single volume day: 3,115,805,723 shares.

**2006**     In March the NYSE Group, Inc., a for-profit, publicly-owned company, is formed out of the merger of the NYSE and Archipelago Holdings, Inc. The merger is the largest-ever among securities exchanges.

# One

# Introduction

Stocks and the markets in which they are traded are important parts of our personal finances and national economies. Today more people than ever own stocks directly, or indirectly through mutual funds, 401k programs, or pension plans. In the bigger picture, stock markets offer individuals and institutions a means to build wealth or reduce risk of financial loss. The increasingly complex web of financial transactions that characterize today's economy often puts stock markets at the center of economic booms and busts. More and more, everyone looks to "the market" for a signal on where the economy is headed.

Stocks represent a retirement nest egg for households and a source of financing for businesses. Without the availability of stocks and the development of financial markets, there would not have been the substantial growth in new businesses created or the growth in our economy. It is, therefore, important for everyone to have a good understanding of stocks and stock markets.

What is a stock? This may sound simple, but it is a useful question to get the discussion rolling. Pick up a finance textbook and it will say that a stock is a financial asset to its owner. It also will say that a stock is a claim against the firm that issued it. Both are correct. When a company issues stock, it acquires funds from those who initially purchase it. Firms sell stock to expand their operations, using the funds to, say, build a new factory or launch a new product line. Once the stock is purchased, however, the firm actually gets no additional funds when the stock is traded over and over. That is, when someone calls a broker and buys a share of Google, the money spent is simply transferred to someone who has decided to sell a share of Google. Once stocks are publicly traded, the issuing firm receives no additional funds.

Even though the firm receives no additional funds from the public trading of its stock, those outstanding shares are claims against the firm. Owning a share of Google gives you some claim over their future profits, and some claim over how the firm is run—shareholders can vote at Google's annual meeting. The former aspect of stock ownership is important because if the firm does well, it is likely that others will want to buy the stock. Since at any one point in time there are only so many shares of stock outstanding, increased demand for a stock drives up its price. For instance, if more and more investors think Google is likely to turn in higher profits, the increased demand for the stock increases its price. For those who bought Google's shares early in this process, as the price increased they became better off: on paper their wealth increased.

It is useful to distinguish at this point the confusion between wealth and income, especially as it relates to the stock market. Wealth refers to the difference between the value of assets and liabilities at a point in time. For example, suppose an individual has 100 shares of XYZ stock, currently priced at $1. Suppose also that they owe $50 to the local bank on a car loan. If that is all the financial assets they own and the loan is the only liability, their wealth is $50, the value of assets (the stock) minus liabilities (the loan). The distinction is that "paper wealth" is not realized until the stock is sold.

Stocks are traded on a number of exchanges and electronic markets, although trading is heading more and more to electronic trading. An exchange usually is thought of as a physical location where traders meet face-to-face to trade stocks. In such an open outcry market, traders announce prices at which to buy stock, or prices at which they are willing to sell. When the two prices are matched, a deal is done. One such market is the New York Stock Exchange (NYSE). Watch any of the financial news networks' wrap of stock market activity, and often a reporter is found on the floor of the exchange, surrounded by people scurrying around. Those people are engaged in trading stocks.

With the advancing technology of trading, the future of markets like the NYSE is limited. Many stock trades today occur not on the floor of a NYSE-type exchange but through an electronic connection between brokers and dealers. This increased sophistication of trading allows information to flow more rapidly and permits trades to be executed quickly. In the United States, an example of such a market is the National Association of Securities Dealers Automated Quotation System (NASDAQ). In the near future, the NYSE also is moving to an electronic format that will reduce activity on its floor.

This brings up an important though sometimes confused point: Stock indexes and stock exchanges or markets are two distinctly different things. The Dow Jones Industrial Average (DJIA) is perhaps the most recognized of the many stock indexes. The value of the DJIA is derived from changes in the prices of the thirty stocks that comprise it. The rise or fall of the index on any

The façade of the New York Stock Exchange, the iconic image of the stock market. Photo courtesy of Corbis.

given day reflects what is happening to the prices of its component stocks, like Wal-Mart or Coca-Cola. The stocks in the DJIA are traded on an exchange, such as the NYSE. There is no market or exchange called the DJIA or, thinking internationally, the FTSE-100. These are indexes that combine stocks that reflect changes in investors' buying and selling. A stock index is not a physical or electronic exchange.

How many exchanges are there? In the United States there are three major exchanges. The most recognizable is the NYSE. This exchange has one of the longest histories in the country and is the one most people think of when referring to "the stock market" today. (A brief history of the NYSE is found in Chapter Two.) The NYSE holds a special place because of its history. The NYSE also is where an average of over 1.6 billion shares of the companies listed on the exchange is traded on a daily basis. The other market that gets attention is the NASDAQ. Unlike the NYSE, the NASDAQ market is electronic: there is no physical exchange. In fact it is the largest electronic securities market in the United States. In this market the stocks of over 3,100 firms are traded, firms that often are associated more with newer technologies. NASDAQ is where companies such as Apple Computer, Inc., Microsoft, and Intel are listed and traded. The other major market is the American Stock Exchange (AMEX). With a history dating from the 1800s, this exchange began literally on the curb outside the more established New York Exchange. Taking the name American Stock Exchange in 1953, the AMEX remains one of the major exchanges in the United States.

What about stock markets in other parts of the world? A brief history of some of the major exchanges, such as stock markets in London, Germany, and Hong Kong is presented in Chapter Seven. Suffice it to say that a simple search reveals that there are almost 150 independent stock exchanges spread across the globe. The list of exchanges literally runs from A to Z: from the Abidjan Exchange to the Zimbabwe Stock Exchange. Indeed, a brief visit to the Internet site www.finix.at indicates that there are links to 145 different stock exchanges. Why so many? That too is a topic for discussion in Chapter Seven. At this point, however, the quick answer is that stock markets represent an efficient way to reallocate financial capital in a country. Without a functioning stock market, how do funds find their way to firms wishing to expand? How do individuals save for the future? The results of research into these questions suggest that having a functioning stock market likely improves a country's chances for faster economic growth.

If there are so many exchanges, how many different stock indexes are there? The answer is hundreds. In the United States alone there are over thirty different stock indexes traded everyday. There is, for example, stocks in the DJIA that was mentioned earlier. More correctly, that DJIA is an index of thirty "industrial" stocks. Industrial is in quotes because the companies listed in the DJIA often are not industrial companies in the traditional sense. Wal-Mart, the nation's largest retailer, would not be considered an industrial company, but it is in the DJIA. Looking at a listing of the DJIA companies over time (available in the Appendix) reveals how the composition of the index has changed.

Other U.S. indexes include the Down Jones 20 transportation company index, the Dow Jones 15 utility company index, and the Dow Jones 65 composite index, the latter being a broad-based compilation of companies across several industries. There also are the often mentioned Standard & Poors 500 index and the NASDAQ composite index. Other indexes followed by investors include the various Russell indexes (1,000, 2,000, and 3,000 firms), the indexes made up of companies in the AMEX, and even some as narrow as the Philadelphia Semiconductor index. Popular foreign indexes include the London Exchange's Financial Times Stock Exchange 100 Index (FTSE-100) and the Hang Seng Index traded on the Hong Kong Stock Exchange, among others.

Some often ask why there are so many indexes. The simple reason is that each index offers investors a different package of companies that best suits their investment needs. One index may be "riskier" (experience more price volatility) than another and attract one set of investors. Others may prefer to invest in an index known more for long-term appreciation. There also are indexes that allow residents in one country to invest in another country's stocks. The array of stocks and stock indexes from which to choose allows an investor to mold their stock portfolio to suit their needs. If investors think the future looks bright for companies in the technology sector, they could buy individual stocks of such companies or invest in a technology-based index that includes several of these firms. The capability of investing in an index not only increases coverage of the businesses in which to invest—from utilities to transportation to banking—but it also diversifies risk. Investing in an index lessens the risk that invested funds will vanish as they might if invested in only one firm. After all, owning stock in a firm does not guarantee that those funds will be there in the future: firms sometimes do go bankrupt. The disappearance of firms following the crash in 1929 and the more recent post–2000 decline in the market is testimony to the fact that investing in stock is a risky venture. Buying an index helps spread that risk out.

If investing is risky, why do it? This question is like asking why people climb dangerous mountains or bungee-jump off of bridges. Such activity gives them a thrill, a rush, an exhilaration that outweighs the potential calamity. For investors, however, buying into the stock market—a risk-taking activity—is done with the expectation of financial gain. The expectation is that if a stock is bought today, its price will be higher some time in the future when it can be sold and the capital gain realized.

Most individuals working today participate in some type of retirement plan, either through their employer or in a self-directed plan. The reason is that they wish greater financial security in their future. Households in the United States increasingly have turned to the stock market as a source of financial gain. According to *Equity Ownership in America, 2005* published by the Investment Company Institute and the Securities Industry Association (2005), in 2005 nearly 57 million households in the United States report owning stocks. This number represents about one-half of all households. What makes this level of participation even more astounding is that in 1983 only about 16 percent of households held stock. One explanation for this surge in equity ownership is increased use of the stock market as a vehicle for retirement saving, whether indirectly through employer retirement plans or in direct ownership.

A related reason why people invest in stocks is evidenced in the behavior of the market itself. Over the past twenty-five years the return from investing in the stock market has been quite remarkable. Of course, timing is a critical factor in making this statement, as the adjoining figure suggests.

Figure 1.1 shows the daily close of the DJIA for the period since 1950. The top panel shows the actual daily close for the index. Because it rose so dramatically in the 1990s, the increases from 1950 to the mid-1980s are dwarfed

**FIGURE 1.1**
**Dow Jones Industrial Average: Close, 1950–2006**

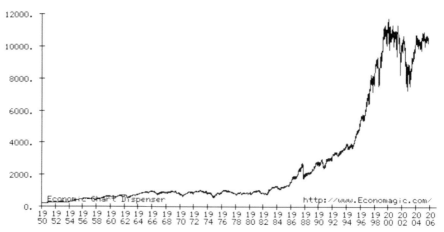

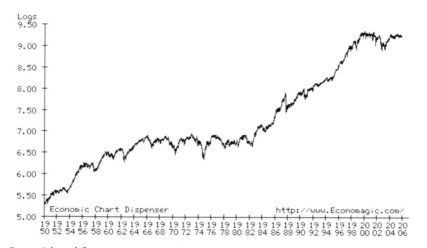

*Source:* Adapted from www.economagic.com.

and appear inconsequential. To adjust for this scaling problem, the bottom panel plots the index using a proportional (logarithmic) scale. This shows the increases in a relative format, indicating that even though the 1990s still stand out, there were some substantial gains—and losses—in the past half-century.

Figure 1.1 shows that the index has been subject to ups and downs, some quite severe. Even if one knew that the market would take a nosedive in 1987, was it wise to invest in stocks back in 1980? The answer is yes, of course. Look at the figure: The level of the DJIA is much higher today, even after the 1987 decline than it was twenty-five years ago. For those investors who bailed out following the 1987 crash—a monumental decline in stock prices at the time, but a small blip in the figure—they missed out on one of the largest and longest bull markets in U.S. history.

But what if someone invested in 1965 with the idea that they had ten years until retirement? The figure also shows that stock prices may not always move upward as smartly as they did since the 1980s. Indeed, the DJIA was about the same value in 1980 as it was in 1965. This means that stock-derived wealth would not have improved very much, if at all. As they say, timing is everything.

The very fact that stocks do not *always* increase in value means that it is very important for potential investors, policymakers, politicians, and average citizens to better understand what the stock market is and how it functions. In the late 1990s, as in the late 1920s, many thought that the stock market was a sure-fire money machine: anyone who invested today would be rich in the future. For some that expectation became a reality. For others, especially those who got into the market in October 1929 or February 2000, they got a different lesson in investing. These two extremes suggest the need to better understand the market for what it is and what it is not. That is the purpose of this book.

# Two

# A Brief History of the U.S.
# Stock Market

A market for stocks in the United States has existed in one form or another for more than 200 years. Originating with a handful of brokers meeting outside on a New York street, the stock market has grown to become one of the most important financial institutions in today's economy. Today there are three major stock exchanges with thousands of firms listed. Along with stocks, there also is a bewildering array of financial products to meet specific investment needs. Indeed, the growth in the stock market and in other financial markets is part of the story about the growth of the U.S. economy.

To fit the vast story of the stock market into one chapter, we focus on the New York Stock Exchange (NYSE). This admittedly ignores the development of other exchanges, such as the American Stock Exchange (AMEX) and the newer electronic markets, such as the National Association of Securities Dealers Automated Quotation (NASDAQ). But the NYSE usually is the market meant when speaking of the stock market in the United States. Thus, referring to "the stock market" hereafter means the NYSE unless stated differently. In addition, to facilitate the discussion movements of the Dow Jones Industrial Average (DJIA), the most widely followed stock price index, will be used almost exclusively.

This treatment omits many of the details that define the development of the stock market. Instead, the focus is on key events that impacted its progress. And when it comes to the stock market, such events are associated most often with historic bull and bear markets—the booms and the busts. Taking this approach captures the broad developments of the stock market, in terms of its institutions and trading activity. It also illustrates those events that led to governmental reactions that largely shape current regulation of the stock market. (Chapter Six provides more details regarding regulation of the stock market.)

## HOW IT ALL STARTED: FROM 1792 TO 1900

The history of the stock market begins in the late 1700s. There was an organized auction market trading mostly commodities on Wall Street in lower New York City during the 1700s. This trading did not include financial securities or stocks as we know them today. This, however, changed dramatically in 1790. In that year Alexander Hamilton, the secretary of the U.S. Treasury, argued for financing the Revolutionary War debt by issuing government securities. Issuance of these securities sparked trading in them in New York and across the country. In addition to these government securities, there was increased trading in a handful of bank stocks. Most notable was trading in the First Bank of the United States and the Bank of New York, the latter a favored enterprise of Hamilton and Aaron Burr, both residents of New York. Indeed, in the early years of trading, Hamilton used his political and financial power to push New York City's financial markets ahead of the rival markets in Boston and Philadelphia.

Trading in securities at the time was unstructured. An auctioneer called out prices for stocks deposited with him for sale. There was no set time or process by which trades took place, or how deals were closed. Trading usually occurred in separate morning and afternoon sessions. In March of 1792 a notice was placed in *Loudon's Register* that stated: "The Stock Exchange Office is opened at No. 22 Wall Street for the accommodation of the dealers in Stock, and in which Public Sales will be held daily at noon as usual in rotation by A. L. Bleeker & Sons, J. Pintard, McEvers and Barclay, Cortlandt & Ferrers, and Jay and Sutton."[1]

Newspapers of the day began to carry reports on sales and prices of the limited number of stocks and securities traded at 22 Wall Street. Business soon improved to the point where traders overflowed the limited space and into the street when weather permitted. The legend is that the favored meeting place for traders was under a large buttonwood (sycamore) tree. Trading covered a variety of financial items, including insurance, securities, and even lottery tickets.[2]

Because the level of competition was increasing and the limited rules of trading often were ignored, some of the brokers created an organization to curtail the rivalry and bring order to the trading process. On May 17, 1792, these brokers finished their deliberations and signed the so-called Buttonwood Agreement. This agreement stated:

We, the subscribers, brokers for the purchase and sale of public stocks, do hereby solemnly promise and pledge ourselves to each other that we will not buy or sell from this date, for any person whatsoever, any kind of public stocks at a less rate than one-quarter of one per cent commission on the specie value, and that we will give preference to each other in our negotiations.

The Buttonwood Agreement is the first official document of the emerging stock exchange. Essentially, the agreement established a club within which stocks were bought and sold between members at specified commissions. Within a year the members would move their burgeoning business indoors, acquiring space in the newly constructed Tontine Coffee House. Although the late 1700s saw the fortunes of the nascent exchange rise and fall, by the early 1800s there was growing interest in trading stocks, even though the majority of trades involved only government securities and bank stocks.

In 1817 another renovation of the exchange's organizational model was made. The New York market was rivaled by the exchange in Philadelphia. The Philadelphia market was so prosperous and successful that a representative from the New York exchange was sent to observe the workings of the Philadelphia market and to report to the membership. Using the Philadelphia exchange as a model, the traders in New York made several changes. Teweles and Bradley note that the first official action was to adopt the name New York Stock and Exchange Board.[3] The traders further cemented their business relationship by signing a constitution, electing officers to guide the Board, and establishing rules for trading. Business henceforth was conducted between 11:30 A.M. and 1:00 P.M. The Board also increased the benefit of membership: trading was carried out *only* by members of the Board, and a broker could be a Board member only if he was elected and paid the initiation fee of $25. In addition to changing how the exchange operated, it relocated to 40 Wall Street. In 1817, the Exchange Board consisted of eight firms with a total of nineteen traders.

The stock market and the Exchange Board experienced more change as the 1800s progressed. In 1835 a fire destroyed the Board's offices forcing yet another move, this time to what would become their permanent location in the Merchant's Exchange Building. The exchange created the office of president in 1842, at the annual salary of $2,000, and then discontinued this position in 1856. By 1848 membership increased to seventy-five traders with over 5,000 shares traded daily.[4]

Improvements in technology dramatically impacted trading. Samuel F. B. Morse, who developed the telegraph in 1832, further improved its applications in the early 1840s. After successfully building several landlines, Morse and his associates started the Magnetic Telegraph Company in 1844. One of the company's first ventures was to build a line between the stock exchanges in New York and Philadelphia. Brokers and traders in both cities then could transmit prices between the two exchanges in a matter of hours, not days. This technological innovation increased the importance of the New York market to the detriment of Philadelphia. Soon New York became the nation's financial capital. Indeed, by the onset of the Civil War, the New York exchange was connected to brokers in every major U.S. city. A price for a stock set on the New York exchange became the stock's price.

Despite setbacks in 1837 and again in 1844, both related to national economic downturns, economic growth kept trading in stocks and the exchange growing. The aforementioned technological advances gave the market a wider appeal, especially geographically. The discovery of gold at Sutter's Mill in 1849 further spurred investment activity as new funds flowed from California gold mines into the New York financial market. Westward expansion continued with a full head of steam, increasing trading activity in railroad stocks to record levels by the 1850s.

Growth in investment activity and the stock market progressed along with the economy. Not unlike the technology boom of the 1990s, investors in the 1850s did not want to be left out of the market for the latest technological advance at the time—railroads.

By the mid-1850s railroad promoters—honest and dishonest alike—were racking up huge debts. Some failed to deliver on promised dividends and this negatively impacted several large financial institutions. One casualty was the Ohio Life Insurance and Trust Company, a firm that did not write insurance policies but served as a depository institution. Heavily invested in railroad stock, problems in the rail industry led to the collapse of Ohio Life in August 1857. Given its size, when Ohio Life failed, it sent a shock wave through the market. Though short-lived, the stock price collapse associated with the failure of Ohio Life and the ensuing Panic of 1857 was one of the most severe in the exchange's history. The good news is that even though stock prices fell sharply, their general decline was short-lived.

After recovering from the events of 1857, stocks faced another setback with the onset of the Civil War. By war's end, however, the market was poised for another upward run. The nature of Wall Street had changed, too. The transformation of the "financial district was far more active than it had been prior to the war," writes Sobel, noting that "most of the stables and many taverns had been replaced by brokerages, insurance offices, and banks. The Wall Street area had jelled, taking on the essential form of a banking-insurance-brokerage complex that characterizes it today."[5] The stock market continued to expand, though not without some significant bumps, throughout the remainder of the 1800s.

Technological innovation continued to expand trading across the country. The electric stock ticker, introduced in 1867, accelerated the transmission

In the 1890s the Dow Jones Industrial Average was dominated by railroads. Photo courtesy of Getty Images/Kim Steele.

of stock price data from the New York market to other exchanges. The telephone found its way to the exchange in 1878, linking traders on the floor to brokerage houses. These developments increased demand for membership on the exchange: By 1869 membership expanded to 1,060 with a seat on the exchange selling for about $7,700. In comparable 2005 dollars, this amounts to $111,594. Compared to the 1817 price, again stated in 2005 dollars, this represents over a 300-fold increase.

The periodic financial panics that occurred before and after the Civil War raised concerns over the exchange's regulation of trading activity. Many in the South saw the New York stock market as a source of its financial problems: Northerners' behavior impacted the South in unexpected and often undesirable ways. The market also was getting a reputation for unbridled speculation, a belief exacerbated by events following the Civil War. For instance, many believe that the failed attempt by the infamous speculator Jay Gould to corner the market for gold led to Black Friday, September 24,

1870. On this day Gould's failure led to a sharp decline in gold prices and with them a decline in stock prices. The aftermath of Gould's speculative misadventure was the financial ruin of many investors.

A cycle of boom and bust characterized the stock market in the late1800s. The market again fell sharply in the late 1870s, and with it success of the exchange. Brokerage houses closed for lack of business and membership prices fell by almost 50 percent. Still, the market and the exchange recovered and expanded, at least until the next distress in financial markets. The Panic of 1893 stands out as one of the more severe downturns in both the economy and the stock market. This boom-bust cycle seemed to occur both in financial markets and the economy. Some argued for a more centralized banking system to help stabilize financial markets. The move to centralize banking regulation and stabilize markets took a major turn in the early 1900s.

## BOOMS AND BUSTS: THE PAST 100 YEARS

The first century of the stock market and the exchange is a colorful history of progress and setback. Rather than present an overview of the market since 1900, it is instructive to focus on four critical episodes that affected the market and its development: the Panic of 1907, the Great Crash of 1929, the Crash of 1987, and the Crash of 2000. Aside from some similarities, the circumstances leading to and following each of these events impacted how the market functions, even today.

### THE PANIC OF 1907

The final decade of the 1800s is often referred to as the "Golden Age" in U.S. economic history. A time of seemingly unbridled economic expansion, tremendous fortunes were made and lost. The names Rockefeller, Carnegie, and Morgan are synonymous with consolidating industries such as steel, railroad, and finance, and creating the so-called trusts that ruled the business and financial landscape. As part of this movement, great investment banks arose, creating the "money trust" of investment and commercial banks, insurance companies. This intermingling of finance and business created a partnership that was not universally welcomed.

Against this backdrop of economic expansion and commercial largess, the Progressive movement gathered momentum. Taking some of their platform from the fading populist movement that had vaulted William Jennings Bryan to national prominence, the Progressives were led by Theodore Roosevelt. Known popularly as a "trust buster," Roosevelt's administration reined in the activities of the industrial and financial giants.

As part of this trust busting, several landmark pieces of legislation were passed and court decisions handed down that affected the stock market. In 1906 the Pure Food and Drug Act and the Hepburn Act were passed to strengthen the oversight powers of the federal government's Interstate Commerce Commission and to restrict what railroads could transport, respectively. Perhaps the most dramatic action took place in August 1907 when Judge Kennesaw Mountain Landis announced that Standard Oil of Indiana would be fined $29,400,000 (over $612 million in 2005 dollars) for illegally accepting rebates from its customers. Since Standard Oil of Indiana's assets totaled only $10 million, the fine fell on its parent company, Standard Oil of New Jersey. This ruling marked the beginning of the decline for John D. Rockefeller's Standard Oil empire and cast a pall over the stock market.

Events of late 1906 and early 1907 sent a chill through the stock market as shown in Figure 2.1. (In all figures in this chapter, the vertical shaded bars mark periods of recession. The dates are based on those established by the National Bureau of Economic Research (NBER) and generally are considered the "official" recession dates.) Stock prices, here measured by the Dow Jones Industrial Average (DJIA), increased sharply following a 1903 swoon. For 1904 the index posted a 42 percent gain. Trading in early 1906 pushed the DJIA above 100 for the first time in its history and the market held its value through 1906. In early 1907, however, a serious change in

**FIGURE 2.1**
**Dow Jones Industrial Average: Close, 1900–1910**

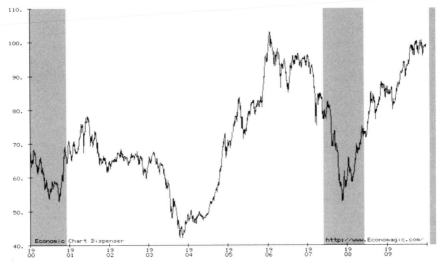

*Source:* Adapted from www.economagic.com.

investors' expectations took hold following the rulings cited above. They began to question future business profits, and there was growing concern about the weakness in the banking institutions that were financing the boom.

A series of downward stock price adjustments began in the spring of 1907. A key factor in this downward shift of stock prices was uncertainty about the Union Pacific railroad company. The Interstate Commerce Commission opened hearings in early 1907 into the activities of financer Edward Harriman. The focus was on Harriman's trading of rail stock, especially since he held controlling interests in several rail companies. Harriman was attempting to control terminal facilities in many cities, which, with his control of Union Pacific, would effectively give him control of rail traffic in the United States. Although the hearings lasted only a few days, investors' uncertainty about Union Pacific was heightened and its stock suffered.

On top of the increase in rumors about speculation and market manipulation, growth of the economy was slowing. The peak of the economic expansion is dated May1907, although individuals at the time would not have known this. But they would have seen the effects, especially the increased withdrawal of bank deposits as individuals sought the safety of cash, the reversal of gold imports, the mounting cost of reconstruction following the 1906 San Francisco earthquake that sapped funds for stock investment, and the fact that foreign stock markets were turning down. Throughout the summer, stock prices rode upon a swirl of rumor and mounting bad economic news. By mid-summer U.S. Steel reported reductions in output, and earnings by railroad companies were faltering.

All of the uncertainty came to a head in October. At the Union Pacific's annual stockholders' meeting, Harriman vowed to expose fellow financer Stuyvesant Fish as a stock manipulator. At the same time, F. Augustus Heinze's attempt to corner the market for United Copper stock failed. This celebrated case in failed stock manipulation caused the price of United Copper to soar past $62 on October 14 only to plunge to $15 two days later. Heinze's failure exposed weakness in other financial firms, especially Mercantile National Bank. The dire news caused customers of Mercantile to begin withdrawing their deposits at an alarming rate. Even though the New York Clearing House—an association of banks organized to support members in times of financial stress—pledged to support Mercantile, public confidence in banking was shaken. Within the next few weeks, other banks also faced massive withdrawals of deposits. Some ultimately closed. The most notable of these was the Knickerbocker Trust Company. The Knickerbocker was one of the largest trusts in New York with about 18,000 depositors and over $62 million in deposits. Knickerbocker was controlled by Charles T. Barney, a well-known associate of Charles W. Morse, who connived with

Heinze in the scheme to corner the market for United Copper stock. This connection did not buoy market confidence in the firm and after several days of heavy deposit losses, Knickerbocker closed its doors for business on October 22.

The stock market responded predictably with a massive sell-off. Although the DJIA had already lost over one-third of its value since the beginning of the year, following the collapse of Knickerbocker and other large trusts the market fell even further. Between October 21 and November 15, the Dow declined from sixty to fifty-three, about 12 percent in a single month. By mid-November the market was down about 44 percent for the year. As shown in Figure 2.1, even though the market turned around late in the year, it lost over 37 percent of its value in 1907.

In the vacuum of any governmental response, J. Pierpont Morgan personally organized a rescue of several New York City banks and financial institutions. Morgan's consortium decided to let Knickerbocker fail, but infused funds into another large troubled firm, Trust Company of America. This rescue was announced concurrently with U.S. treasury secretary George Cortelyou's statement that the Treasury would deposit $25 million in New York banks to meet any further emergencies. An infusion of funds by Morgan and his associates into the stock market also helped troubled brokerage houses remain afloat. Although there were several stressful days in late October, the financial rescue mission led by Morgan helped turn the stock market around. Not only did banks soon reopen for business, but the market also began to gain ground. By year's end the DJIA increased about 11 percent and continued its ascent for the next couple of years (see Figure 2.1). By the end of 1909 the DJIA was back to levels not seen for several years.

The Panic of 1907 came to a relatively quick end. Without the intervention of J. P. Morgan, the outcome may have been much different, however. This was not lost on government officials, especially those who believed that the economic development of the country and the intermittent financial crises called for restructuring the banking system. The 1907 crisis gave rise to a series of legislative efforts to create a central bank. Congress commissioned an enormous study of the entire financial system, leading to countless hearings and many multivolume studies. In the end, the Federal Reserve Act was produced and signed by President Woodrow Wilson on December 31, 1913.

The Panic of 1907 also increased government scrutiny of the stock market and especially those who tried to manipulate stock prices. The Hughes Committee of New York investigated the activities of banks, insurance companies, and exchange operations. The committee called for the exchange to require listed companies to file periodic statements of financial condition, including balance sheets and income statements. The exchange also instituted some changes, but they obviously were not sufficient to curb the speculative zeal that increased stock prices in the 1920s.

One reaction to the events of 1907 was the founding in 1908 of the New York Curb Agency, a group of street brokers. These brokers formed a Listing Department and, in 1911, opened a central office from which business was conducted. Forty years later, in 1953, the Curb Agency was renamed the American Stock Exchange.

### THE ROARING TWENTIES AND THE CRASH OF 1929

The 1920s was a spectacular decade in the United States on several fronts. Coming out of a severe recession following World War I, the economy boomed. By the mid-1920s, employment was up nearly 20 percent, reaching over 30 million employed in 1926. The number of business concerns also showed marked growth, increasing about 12 percent between 1921 and 1926. All of this activity is summarized by looking at the growth in real income: Between 1921 and 1926, real national income in the United States jumped nearly 37 percent, or at an average annual rate of more than 7 percent.

Along with the good economic news came bustling financial markets. Some of the apparent successes were based on questionable foundations, however. The most notable was the Florida real estate boom. During the mid-1920s, as northern residents began to look south for warmer winter climates and retirement retreats, unscrupulous Florida real estate developers cashed in. They played not only on the willingness of the newly wealthy to spend the paper profits they had made in the stock market, but also on the fact that many were willing to buy properties—sight unseen. Property values ranged from $8,000 to over $75,000 (in 1920s dollars) depending on whether you located inland or sought ocean-front property. Unfortunately for buyers, some of it was swamp either way.

As the hurricanes of 2005 demonstrated yet again, weather-related catastrophes have a way of curtailing real estate booms. In 1926 a hurricane swept through Florida and the real estate boom was over. Even as investors realized that their investments suddenly were worthless, the curious fact was that the collapse of the Florida real estate market did not dampen other investors' belief in getting rich. In his classic *The Great Crash: 1929*, John Kenneth Galbraith observes that during the 1920s, "the faith of Americans in quick, effortless enrichment in the stock market was becoming everyday more evident."[6] While troubles in the Sunshine State raised eyebrows about the financial industry in general, it was mostly passed off as an isolated event, something that should not be interpreted as a general condition.

If this suggests that the market took absolutely no notice of the events down South, that is true. Looking at Figure 2.2 the market dipped in 1926 after a fairly steady increase that began in early 1924. This interruption in the market's upward move was brief, however. If you had invested in stocks in 1924, three years later, even with the 1926 dip, your nest egg was about 50 percent larger.

The stock market's rise in the late 1920s was anything but smooth. After a substantial increase in 1927, stock prices were quite choppy in 1928. In the early months of the year, stocks surged ahead on heavy trading volume. By early summer, however, retreating stock prices prompted financial and political leaders to provide soothing words to assuage worried investors. Andrew W. Mellon, the secretary of the U.S. Treasury, opined that all was well and that "the high tide of prosperity will continue."[7] Herbert Hoover was elected president in November 1928, and stock prices and trading volume surged. Indeed, 1928 ranks as the third best year ever in terms of percentage gain in the DJIA. Viewed as a pro-business president, investors jumped quickly to buy stocks before the rally passed them by.

Trading in stocks increased by leaps and bounds in 1928 and early 1929. So did trading on margin. Margin trading—buying stocks with borrowed money—allowed many investors to leverage a few dollars into thousands of

**FIGURE 2.2**
**Dow Jones Industrial Average: Close, 1910–1935**

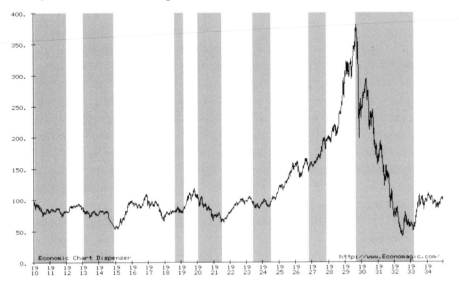

*Source:* Adapted from www.economagic.com.

dollars in stock purchases. By investing a small portion of their own money and borrowing the rest from bankers, every rise in stock prices increased the expected return many times over. As long as stock prices rose, banks did not call in the loans. To get some perspective on this practice, brokers' loans increased about 63 percent between the end of 1927 and November 1928. This surge in margin buying and the acquiescence by the regulatory authorities, especially the Federal Reserve, fueled an even greater increase in stock prices during 1929.

It is not so much that the Federal Reserve shirked its responsibilities as it sent conflicting signals to the market participants. Fed officials warned that stock prices were getting ahead of the so-called fundamentals. Even so, the Federal Reserve allowed banks to borrow funds through its discount window at the low rate of 5 percent (it was increased from 3.5 percent to 5 in an ill-fated effort to stem speculative borrowing) and lend it out as margin loans at an interest rate upward of 12 percent.

In light of such speculative arbitrage with borrowed funds, the Federal Reserve acted in early 1929 to curb speculative activity in the stock market. Raising the discount rate further in August and increasing the margin requirement for borrowing funds to invest in stocks, the Fed sent an important message. By its actions the Fed sought to shine light directly on the 1929 version of irrational exuberance. Like the Fed seventy years later, it did little more than that, however. Earlier in its September 1928 *Bulletin* the Fed stated that it "neither assumes the right nor has it any disposition to set itself up as an arbiter of security speculation or values."[8]

Part of the confusion over Fed policy arose from the fact that Charles E. Mitchell, a director of the Federal Reserve Bank of New York and a top executive of the financial firm National City, made many public pronouncements that seemed at odds with official Fed positions. For example, while the Fed suggested that funds borrowed from the discount window should not be used for speculative purposes, Mitchell's bank stated in its monthly newsletter that "the Federal Reserve Banks . . . wish to avoid a general collapse of the securities markets."[9] For Mitchell and many other observers, averting a crisis in the financial markets meant that the Fed should not do anything that would halt the run-up in stock prices. Why? Because such actions could lead to a severe decline in general business conditions, not to mention the value of stock portfolios held by many. In the final analysis, the Federal Reserve basically stood on the sidelines as the events of 1929 unfolded.

In late 1928 the DJIA fluctuated around 300 (see Figure 2.2). The year 1929 opened with another surge in prices. If not already remembered as the year of "The Crash," 1929 could have gone down as the year of unbridled optimism. In spring of 1929 John J. Raskob, the chairman of the Democratic National Committee, wrote in the *Ladies Home Journal* that any average individual could put money into an investment trust—a financial company that specialized in leveraging a few dollars into many more—and get rich in the ongoing stock boom. The famous financier Bernard Baruch suggested that the economy was on the verge to take off. Princeton University professor Irving Fisher joined the chorus with his learned opinion that stock prices had reached a permanently higher plateau and could only go higher.

The pundits of the day even suggested that the Federal Reserve, through its veiled warnings about overpriced stocks, was simply getting in the way of progress. In what must be one of the most ill-timed treatises on Fed policy, Joseph Stagg Lawrence wrote in 1929 that "It must be evident that the consensus of judgment of the millions whose valuations function on that admirable market, the Stock Exchange, is that stocks are not at present prices overvalued. . . . Where is that group of men with the all-embracing wisdom which will entitle them to veto the judgment of this intelligent multitude?"[10] His solution to bad Fed policy was simple: "Wall Street should patronize only banks without the [Federal Reserve] system. As a Community it has ample financial strength to be independent of a central bank which has demonstrated its unenlightened and militant provincialism."[11]

A minority of experts warned of a coming financial debacle. Paul Warburg, then at the International Acceptance Bank and an early advocate for creating the Federal Reserve System, warned that continued speculation would bring a collapse in stock prices and in the economy. Editorial writers for various financial publications agreed. Poor's *Weekly Business and Investment Letter* posted warnings about overpriced securities. The *New York Times* financial page editor argued for cooler heads in this time of increasingly frenzied trading.

Although stock prices trended downward in late summer, it was a speech given by the well-respected financial advisor Roger Babson that first shook the market. Even though many editorial writers and commentators suggested that stock prices had gotten too high, Babson's prediction that stock prices were long-past due for a correction got everyone's attention. His timing was impeccable: His warning combined with the Fed's tightening and the slowing in economic growth created conditions that were ripe for a downward revision in stock prices. (The NBER dates August 1929 as the peak of the business cycle.) By the end of August the DJIA was at 384 and by the end of September it stood at 349. Sometimes referred to as the "Babson break," this decline was only a modest decline compared to what would transpire in the following month.

A quick glance at Figure 2.2 reveals the sharp break in October 1929 that marks the onset of the Great Crash. The DJIA already had declined over 25 percent from its August level. Still, as October unfolded, a number of events continued to negatively impact market psychology and stock prices. Trading volume in October began to swell to record levels. By Monday, October 21, trading was so heavy that the ticker lagged by an hour. The fact that the ticker could not keep up with transactions meant that investors lacked reliable information about the direction of prices. Traders did not know if they were buying stocks that in reality were priced higher or lower than when they purchased them a few hours earlier. This breakdown in information flow caused some panic selling and prompted financial leaders to calm jittery nerves. Irving Fisher publicly suggested that such heavy trading was simply "shaking out the lunatic fringe."[12]

By Wednesday, October 23, the market suffered continued losses on heavy trading volume. The ticker again was delayed and massive selling became common. Even the blue-chip stocks suffered heavy losses as investors tried to unload their holdings. Comments by notable individuals, such as George Mitchell of National City, were not sufficient to reverse the market's downward momentum.

October 24, 1929, will forever be known as Black Thursday. On that day over 13 million shares were traded, more than four times the average daily volume. Several large banks quickly organized to buy stocks hoping to prevent further declines. Included in this "organized support" of the market were National City Bank, Chase National Bank, and the Guaranty Trust Company. Even officials of J. P. Morgan and Company, this time lacking the leadership of its namesake, joined the effort. By the day's end, their organized purchase gave stocks a boost. On Friday there was further effort to support stock prices. Officials of banks, trust companies, and insurance companies, not to mention government officials, touted the market's resilience and the economy's underlying strength.

This reassurance did not resuscitate the market. On Monday, October 28, the market opened down and trading quickly overwhelmed the ticker. As Galbraith describes it, "Support, organized or otherwise, could not contend with the overwhelming, pathological desire to sell."[13] On Black Monday there was no late-day rally to calm investors' nerves: The DJIA fell by 13 percent that day. The next day—Black Tuesday—the stock index declined an additional 12 percent. October 28 and 29, 1929, rank as the second and third, respectively, worse percentage point loss days in the history of the index.

The *New York Times* headline for Tuesday, October 29, said it all: "Stock Prices Slump $14,000,000,000 in Nation-Wide Stampede to Unload; Bankers to Support Market Today." This stampede lasted for several days. Not only were the trading floor and back rooms of the exchange chaotic, but when the news spread, out-of-town banks also called in loans from their East-Coast correspondents. This put further pressure on the financial system and a stock market whose success had grown to rely largely on leveraged funds. Margin calls came in faster than stocks could be liquidated, large trust companies attempted to unload stocks, and rumors spread that the banker pool that had tried to support stocks was now selling like everyone else.

By November 1929 the DJIA was about 50 percent of its August value. Interestingly, as shown in Figure 2.2, stock prices stabilized and even rose slightly before year's end. This revival was short-lived, however. Beginning in early 1930 stock prices began a long and protracted descent over the next few years. By late 1932 the DJIA was lower than it had been anytime since 1920. Indeed, in percentage terms, three of the ten worst years for the DJIA occurred in the early 1930s. Along with the percentage change, these years are 1930 (−34 percent), 1931 (−53 percent), and 1932 (−23 percent). Although the Great Crash was over, it took many years for stock prices to regain the ground lost.

The Panic of 1907 helped usher in the reforms that created the Federal Reserve. The Crash of 1929 and the Great Depression also gave rise to many reforms, this time with special emphasis on how the stock market operated and its relation to banking. The Banking Act of 1933 affected the banking-stock market relation. In addition, legislation aimed specifically at reforming how the market operated was passed in the early 1930s. Two key pieces of legislation are the Securities Act of 1933 and the Securities and Exchange Act of 1934. Although a detailed discussion is left for Chapter Six, these changes came in the wake of massive fraud and stock price manipulation in the market. In all, they attempted to raise the regulatory barriers for such behavior and to improve the flow of information to investors. These laws established the foundation for stock market regulation in the United States and in many other countries.

## THE CRASH OF 1987: COULD IT HAPPEN AGAIN?

On Tuesday, October 20, 1987, the headline of the *New York Times* related the previous day's financial calamity: "Stocks Plunge 508 Points, A Drop of 22.6%; 604 Million Volume Nearly Doubles Record." Another article on the front page stated the question that leaped to everyone's mind: "Does 1987 Equal 1929?" As readers across the country and around the world tried to digest the news, little did they know that while another "Black Monday" marked the onset of the 1987 crash, the stock market nearly ceased to operate the next day.

Was 1987 like 1929? In some ways the answer is yes. In percentage terms, the October 19, 1987, drop exceeded that of October 28, 1929: 22.6 versus 12.8. In other ways, however, the two crashes are distinctly different. What made the 1987 crash much different than 1929 was the response of the

Federal Reserve. Indeed, it is testament to their response in 1987 that not only was there no "great depression" in the wake of the 1987 crash, but the economy suffered only a brief slowdown in its growth.

Figure 2.3 shows the behavior of the DJIA in the decade of the 1980s. Compared to the 1920s (Figure 2.2), both market expansions begin in the aftermath of a severe economic recession: The recession of 1982–84 is (thus far) the worst recession in the post–World War II period. Although there are competing theories, most observers agree that one reason for the rise in stock prices in the 1980s stems from the massive number of initial public offerings (IPOs) and corporate takeovers using leveraged buyouts. In the first quarter of 1983 corporations offered almost $9 million in new stock, up nearly 380 percent from a year earlier.[14] Even with an economy coming out of recession, this is staggering. Another impetus to stock prices came from the other side of the market, not in new offerings but in activities that reduced the amount of stock in circulation: corporate takeovers.

The nature of the 1980s boom gave rise to two infamous characters. One is Ivan Boesky. Boesky started his own company in the mid-1970s and over the next few years the company grew in the relatively new area of risk arbitrage. Boesky and his associates became some of the most influential and powerful individuals on Wall Street and in corporate America. In the mid-1980s it was reported that the firm managed a pool of financial assets then valued at over

**FIGURE 2.3**
**Dow Jones Industrial Average: Close, 1980–1990**

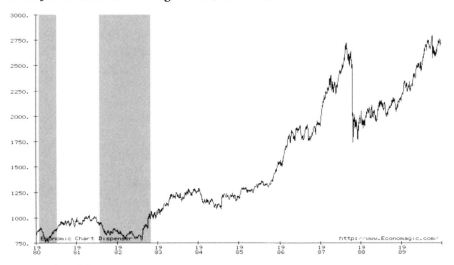

*Source:* Adapted from www.economagic.com.

$2 billion. It appears, however, that the success of Boesky and his firm arose in part from violating the Securities and Exchange rules. In November 1986 Boesky settled charges of insider trading with a fine of about $100 million. Boesky's shining star quickly extinguished.

The name most often associated with the frenzied 1980s takeover market is Michael Milken, then an employee of Drexel, Burnham Lambert. Milken became known as the "king of junk bonds." A junk bond is simply a bond rated as "speculative": that is, even though the bond carries a high potential rate of return, it also has a much higher probability of default. Milken believed that the gap between rates on speculative bonds and better quality (less risky) bonds was larger than relative default risk alone could explain. He convinced many corporate clients that he was correct.

Milken's use of junk bonds revolutionized the takeover process. Using junk bonds to finance takeovers, mergers, or corporate restructuring, firms issued much more debt to finance their activities. In essence, junk bonds made takeovers cheaper. Leveraged buyouts using junk bonds became the rage in the 1980s because companies could get so much for seemingly so little. For example, the average leveraged buyout might use 25–30 percent of its funding from junk bonds, 10 percent from equity, and the rest from senior-grade debt. Changing the corporate landscape became financially attractive in ways that no one could believe. Although corporate takeovers and leveraged buyouts continued even after the market crash in 1987, the bottom fell out of the market. A rise in junk bond defaults, rising interest rates, and a number of civil and criminal convictions against Milken and Drexel halted (temporarily) the wave of mergers. In the end, Milken did time and paid a huge fine; Drexel ceased to exist.

One way in which the merger mania influenced the stock market was that absorbing other companies often reduced the number of shares available for trading. Many companies during the 1980s went private by purchasing their own outstanding stock. The overall consequence was a smaller supply of stock facing an increasing demand by investors. The economics of this combination resulted in an increase in the general level of stock prices, illustrated by the advancing DJIA in Figure 2.3.

Even though it is estimated that nearly one-fifth of the U.S. population directly owned stock by 1987, the boom of the 1980s was driven largely by institutional investors.[15] A spin-off of the buyout-merger activity, insurance companies, mutual funds, and pension fund managers all were heavily participating in the market. The increase from the demand side and the limited amount of stock purchase pushed stock prices higher. New technologies being introduced facilitated trading. These included not only computerized systems that sped up the actual transacting of buys and sells, but also the use of computer programs to signal the "best" times to buy or sell—so-called program trading. Improved transacting technology and the increased reliance on mathematical models to trigger the buying and selling of huge blocks of stock (and futures, of which more will be said shortly) proved to be a combination that, like margin buys in the 1920s, pushed Wall Street into ever more vigorous trading. This new trading style, reminiscent of the 1920s, led to wider swings in stock prices and increased trading volume.

By late 1986 concerns about the impact of computerized trading systems were being raised by, among others, John J. Phelan, chairman of the New York Stock Exchange. Most firms and traders on the street ignored such concerns. "In the remaining months of 1986 and through most of 1987," writes Metz, "Wall Street firms will become more aggressive in their in-dex arbitrage, and more and more of their clients will ask to get on the bandwagon . . . . The trend will also be driven by another evolving program trading strategy, 'dynamic hedging,' more widely known by the misnomer 'portfolio insurance.' "[16] Some argue that it was not program trading that caused the October 1987 break but the failure of the actual trading mech-anism. That is, because program trading involves movements of huge blocks of stock, an atypically large volume could overwhelm the trading network. Even with continual technological improvements to facilitate trading, by Oc-tober 1987 the confluence of tremendous trading volume (stemming in part to activity in the Chicago Mercantile Exchange) and the inability by floor specialists to establish orderly markets led to one of the most dramatic breaks in the stock market's history.

When the DJIA reached its then record high of 2,722.4 in August 1987, this marked a near-doubling of stock prices in only a few short years (see Figure 2.3). Even though the DJIA stumbled a bit earlier in the year, stock prices continued to rise even in the face of unfavorable economic news. The U.S. trade deficit was soaring and the dollar's exchange value with foreign currencies was dropping. Under the leadership of its newly installed chairman Alan Greenspan, the Fed was pushing interest rates higher in part to protect the weak dollar. Just before Labor Day the Fed announced that it was raising its key policy tool, the federal funds rate, by fifty basis points. This an-nouncement sent a shock wave through the market. "With stocks already looking too expensive relative to bonds," Metz notes, "the Fed suddenly and substantially enhanced the allure of bonds."[17] Following the Fed's rate hike, stock prices began to recede from their August highs.

Not only was the economic data unfavorable, but the federal government publicly began taking a closer interest in the buyout activity that helped fuel the market's advance. On Tuesday, October 13, the House Ways and Means Committee announced it was going to investigate the tax benefits associated with leveraged buyouts. The message was clear: Congress intended to close some loopholes through which the corporations and Wall Street firms had wiggled. Congress wanted to get its share of the taxes that it had missed. With rising interest rates and the threatened loss of tax advantages for buyouts and mergers, the drop in stock prices accelerated.

What makes this part of the story different from 1929 is how the market dropped. For example, the day after the Ways and Means Committee announcement, the DJIA lost ninety-five points. This decline did not come from ordinary investors selling their stock but from sell orders emanating from the Chicago Mercantile Exchange (CME). Futures contracts for the S&P 500 were sold by traders in Chicago and this translated into selling pressure in the stock exchange back in New York. (This relation is detailed in Chapter Five.) Further selling of futures contracts pushed the DJIA down farther on Thursday, October 15, when it closed at 2,355. In just a little more than six weeks the DJIA lost about 13 percent from its peak value. The worst was yet to come, however.

Trading on Friday, October 16, opened with the news that an oil tanker traveling under the U.S. flag was attacked by Iranian forces. Fears of increased turmoil in the Middle East and the potential disruption of oil flows triggered sell orders as investors sought safety in bonds and cash. In the late morning a handful of index arbitrageurs executed sell programs in the NYSE that amounted to over $180 million. This action created a large discount between the S&P 500 futures contract and the S&P index value in New York, and this deviation activated a number of program trades to sell. Metz estimates that program trading accounted for 43 percent of the volume in the final half hour.[18] By the close, the DJIA had lost another 108 points.

Modern technology made trading faster and more efficient. Even so, trading on Monday, October 19, opened with a problem familiar to investors in 1929: a slowdown of price information. In 1987, unlike 1929, the ticker was not delayed, but trading was delayed because of order imbalances with the specialists on the floor of the exchange. The specialists at the NYSE confronted huge sell orders stemming from the actions at the CME. With sell orders outnumbering buy orders, the NYSE imposed trading delays. These delays meant that providing information about market clearing prices—the specialists' job—slowed. This lack of information—the modern version of the delayed ticker tape—further raised anxiety levels of traders at the CME. Try as they might, specialists faced a losing battle that day, also known as Black Monday. John J. Phelan later recalled it as "the nearest thing to a meltdown I ever want to see." On Monday, October 19, 1987, over 604 million shares were traded, a bit less than the previous record set on the previous Friday. When it was over, the DJIA lost 508 points or 22.6 percent, making it by far the worst percentage decline day in the stock market's history.

On Monday night there was a scramble for liquidity. Because some specialists ended the day as net buyers of stock, they could not meet their purchases with existing funds (transactions must be cleared within five days). Normal providers of funding now stalled; banks denied loan commitments and withheld credit from the market. The situation was so dire that one firm merged *overnight* with another brokerage house to meet its financial responsibilities. Not only did Monday reveal that the specialists could not handle such market pressure, but it also exposed trouble in the existing technology of trading. The breakdown in the system meant that stop-loss orders could not be executed. Unable to get through to brokers, many traders lost huge sums simply because they could not execute their sell orders.

Trading on Tuesday, October 20, was delayed and trading in many stocks, when the market finally opened, was halted at times. One early event marks a clear difference between the 1929 and 1987 crashes. Early Tuesday morning the Federal Reserve released the following statement: "The Federal Reserve, consistent with the responsibilities as the nation's central bank, affirmed today its readiness to serve as a source of liquidity to support the economic and financial system." The fact that the Fed immediately lowered the federal funds rate from 7.50 percent to 6.75 percent helped turn market psychology around. Behind the scenes arm twisting by Fed officials, most notably Chairman Greenspan and Gerald Corrigan, president of the Federal Reserve Bank of New York, helped. Stocks closed higher on Tuesday than Monday and by Wednesday, the DJIA posted a 10 percent gain. The Fed's actions during the rest of October were aimed at restoring confidence in the market. As illustrated in Figure 2.3, the DJIA regained its balance, closing the year without further major losses.

The aftermath of the 1987 crash bears no resemblance to the events following 1929. Not only was there no economic depression, there was not even a mild recession. This surprised many observers (and many professional economists) who predicted that such loss of wealth would reduce consumer spending and lead to an overall economic downturn. This reaction, or lack of, is partly explained by the rapid response of the Federal Reserve. As just discussed, the Fed in 1987 moved quickly to fulfill its role as lender of last resort: in times of financial crises injecting liquidity into the market, arm twisting financial institutions, and standing ready to insure an orderly market. Robert T. Parry, president of the Federal Reserve Bank of San Francisco, summarized the Fed's actions as doing "what it was supposed to do: it transferred the systematic risk from the market to the banks and ultimately to the Fed, which is the only financial institution with pockets deep enough to bear this risk. This allowed the market intermediaries to perform their usual functions and helped keep the market open."[19] The 1987 crash brought about a number of institutional reforms in the stock market. Most of these related to stopping trading when certain volume barriers were breached. These "circuit breakers" served to coordinate trading halts across the futures and equity markets. It became widely believed that selling pressure emanating from the equity futures market in Chicago and the inability of the trading mechanism to handle the deluge of sell orders explained the crash. The objective of circuit breakers was to halt trading so the second of these events could not occur.

When looking at the long history of stock prices, the Crash of 1987 looks like a blip in the market rally that began in the early 1980s and ran until 2000. Charles Schwab, the namesake of the brokerage house, said that "Black Monday [1987] did to investors what *Jaws* did to swimmers. They do not want to go in the water, but they still come to the beach."[20] Their fear of the water was short-lived. By 1990, the DJIA passed through 2,800, surpassing the peak reached in August 1987. As the 1990s wore on, investors forgot about Black Monday and dove back into the financial waters with even greater enthusiasm.

### THE CRASH OF 2000: NEW ECONOMY OR IRRATIONAL EXUBERANCE?

At the close of 1996 Alan Greenspan, chairman of the Federal Reserve's Board of Governors, delivered the Francis Boyer Lecture to an assembled dinner crowd at the American Enterprise Institute, a Washington, D.C. think-tank. The title of the speech was typical for such gatherings: The Challenge of Central Banking in a Democratic Society. In his wide-ranging talk about the pitfalls and dilemmas facing central bankers like himself, the chairman uttered two words that to many captured the essence of the ongoing run-up in stock prices: "Irrational exuberance." What he actually said was "But how do we know when irrational exuberance has unduly escalated asset values, which become subject to unexpected and prolonged contractions as they have in Japan over the past decade?"

Embedded within a speech of over 4,300 words, these two words caused quite a stir and remain part of our vocabulary. Stock market participants now believed that the chief U.S. monetary policymaker thought stocks were overpriced. The thinly veiled hint was clear: If no correction occurred, there would likely be a sustained bear market or even another stock market crash like 1987. As Greenspan made clear only a few sentences later, a "collapsing asset bubble" would have dire economic consequences, as the recent Japanese experience had showed. Greenspan had thrown down the gauntlet to those who believed that stock prices would only continue to rise.

History informs us that stock prices did in fact continue to rise for the rest of the decade. Figure 2.4 shows this quite vividly. Within a few years of this speech Greenspan began to explain the continued ascent of stock prices with

**FIGURE 2.4**
**Dow Jones Industrial Average: Close, 1990–2005**

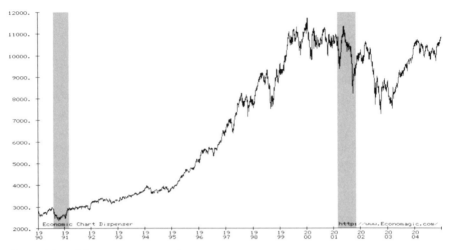

*Source:* Adapted from www.economagic.com.

reference to a "new economy." What are some of the reasons for the market's unprecedented rise and some explanations for the decline that began in early 2000? Was the eventual crash the bursting of an asset bubble, or was it a predictable correction from changes in the underlying fundamentals?

The majority of economists believe that individuals in financial markets behave rationally. There may be times when stock prices appear to lose track of the underlying fundamentals, such as corporate earnings and profits, that explain stock prices, but they are isolated instances. If stock prices are explained by investors' perceptions of future or expected cash flows being generated by companies, then the run-up in prices during the 1990s was tailor-made to fit the "fundamentals" view.

Although many thought the Crash of 1987 would adversely affect the economic expansion, the economy continued to grow throughout the 1990s. Except for a relatively mild recession in 1990, the period from the early 1980s through the end of the 1990s is characterized by sustained economic growth. One economist even dubbed the period "the long boom." But what separates this period of economic expansion from others was a suitable explanation. For many the expansion occurred because the long-awaited revolution in information technology (IT) had finally taken hold. Although economists predicted that the improvements in computer technology and the attendant increase in the use of computers would spur productivity and economic activity, it never seemed to materialize. That is, until the mid-1990s.

A recognized expert on the relation between capital formation and economic growth observed in 2001 that "the resurgence of the American economy since 1995 has outrun all by the most optimistic expectations. . . . The development and deployment of information technology is the foundation of the American growth resurgence."[21] This view reiterated what many already suspected: computers and related technologies had achieved something of a quantum leap. They were faster, more capable, and their use to gather and process information reached new levels. As the IT revolution took off, the economy (and stock prices) went along for the ride.

Not only did the economy grow and incomes rise, but inflation also remained surprisingly subdued. Unlike past economic expansions that brought higher rates of inflation, this time prices did not increase very rapidly. Some explained this phenomenon by the fact that improved communications and computerization lowered operating costs of firms, cost savings that got passed along in the form of slower price increases. Large box stores like Wal-Mart and Costco took advantage of the information technology to significantly improve their handling of inventory and shipping, both of which allowed them to realize significant cost savings. Another idea was that increased global competition forced U.S. producers to hold down price increases.

If stock prices reflect investors' expectations of firms' future earnings, a growing economy explains some of the upward march in stock prices. As Figure 2.4 shows, however, the second half of the 1990s was distinctly different from the first half. Even though the market was rising at a reasonably healthy pace following the 1987 crash, it exploded after 1995. In late December 1991 the DJIA broke through 3,100. It took until February 1995 for it to surpass the 4,000 mark. Using the same time interval, the DJIA went from 4,000 in 1995 to over 11,700 by 2000. Clearly something was different in the second half of the 1990s.

The cost of computing plummeted in the 1990s. Computing was faster and cheaper than ever before, and everyone projected that price declines would continue into the foreseeable future. So how would a market populated by rational investors respond to such rosy forecasts? Investors flocked to buy tech stocks. It made sense to do so. Stanford University economist Robert Hall observed that "a rational stock market measures the value of the property owned by corporations. Some types of corporate property, especially the types held by high-tech companies, have values that are exquisitely sensitive to the future growth of the cash they generate."[22] In other words, the high-flying stock prices on firms that seemed to offer nothing more than possible future success was explained not by invoking a "bubble" explanation, but by investors willing to bet that the stock they just purchased was going to be the next Microsoft or Dell.

The bull market was not without some setbacks, however. The market was impacted, albeit temporarily, by the onset of the Asian Crisis in 1997. (See Figure 2.4.) The crisis was precipitated by speculative attacks on the currencies of several East Asian countries. Beginning with a major devaluation of the Thai baht, the crisis spread to the currencies of other countries, including South Korea, Indonesia, Malaysia, and the Philippines. There are several theories, but the most popular explanation is that the rapid expansion of these economies was built on fraudulent behavior in the banking systems. As the crisis unfolded, it became clear that loans were made not on the basis of expected financial outcomes but often on the basis of a borrower's relation with the bank. As the fraud became apparent, foreign investors unloaded financial assets in these countries and with changes in investment expectations, others followed suit. The speculative attacks began.

The U.S. stock market also was affected more dramatically by two related events in 1998. One was the collapse of the Russian financial system in August 1998. This produced a sharp reaction in the U.S. stock market: On August 31, 1998, the DJIA dropped over 512 points, a 6.4 percent loss on one day. In and of itself, the Russian collapse probably would not have affected stock prices for long. However, the fact that this event caused the near-collapse of a U.S. hedge firm, Long-Term Capital Management (LTCM), makes it worthy of discussion.

The collapse of the Russian financial system—the Russian government essentially declared bankruptcy—caused many investors to reassess the relative risk of corporate and government bonds. In a flight to quality, investors shifted into safer government bonds. Unfortunately for the management of LTCM, this response widened the spread between prices on the two bonds. LTCM had bet on exactly the opposite to occur: Since the spread already was at a higher than normal level, LTCM bet that it would shrink. When the Russian crisis widened the spread even further, LTCM faced huge losses. By mid-September the company was no longer able to meet creditors' demands, and LTCM, like the Russian government, was effectively insolvent. As seen in Figure 2.4, stocks took a beating in mid-1998 as news of Russia and LTCM spread. The DJIA, which had peaked at 9,328 in July, dropped to 7,539 by August 31, 1998.

To meet its obligations, LTCM could have sold off its assets at whatever the market would pay. Such a "fire-sale" of LTCM's assets—nearly $80 billion in securities and $1 trillion in financial derivatives—would negatively impact a market that already was jittery from the problems in Asia and Russia. So the Fed moved quickly and signaled the seriousness of the situation by lowering the federal funds rate seventy-five basis points, a large change given its usual twenty-five basis point changes. The Fed also engineered a very public rescue plan of LTCM by its creditors. This plan infused $3.6 billion into LTCM in exchange for specified changes in management of the fund.

Whether this intervention was a wise policy is debatable, but it did calm financial markets. Stock prices began to climb sharply as the crisis was averted. From its low of 7,539 on August 31, the market once again began its upward climb, with the DJIA pushing through 9,400 by the end of 1998.

As the DJIA pushed through 10,000 in early 1999—it stood at 3,600 only five years earlier—there arose an increasing level of anxiety. As in each of the previous crashes, the period preceding the decline often is characterized by mixed signals from otherwise reputable sources. Recall Irving Fisher's claim on the eve of the 1929 crash that stock prices would only go higher? In an eerily similar statement, financial reporter Gretchen Morgenson wrote in the *New York Times* that "the market's [upward] move is significant in what it reflects: the unparalleled strength of the economy and the dominance of the world economic stage by American Corporations."[23] Juxtapose this view to that of Gail Dudack, the chief market strategist for Warburg, the U.S. unit of UBS, a major investment bank: "Wall Street is moving from fact to fiction."[24] Her view was that the basis for stock valuation simply was not there. Investors were not irrational in trying to find the next Microsoft or Wal-Mart, but the *reported* earnings upon which they based their investment decisions simply were not there to support the high-flying stock prices.

Attempts to explain the markets in the late 1990s did not account for the magnitude of misreported earnings. If market crashes are associated with key events, the massive and oftentimes fraudulent reporting of earnings exposed in 2000 is a good candidate to explain the crash. Speaking before an audience at the Center for Law and Business on the campus of New York University in September 1998, Arthur Levitt, the commissioner of the Securities and Exchange Commission, suggested that "managing may be giving way to manipulation. Integrity may be losing to illusion."[25]

Of course history indicates that misrepresentation of earnings occurred in some of the largest firms traded on the street. While this misrepresentation helped drive stock prices higher, even allowing the fifteen-year-old AOL to swallow the larger and older Time Warner, it would not continue. As 1999 turned into 2000 the "millennium bug" failed to materialize and stock prices began to soften. After a flat first half, stocks in late 1999 began to rise into 2000. The peak in the DJIA was reached on January 14, 2000, when it topped out at 11,722.98. In March 2000 the effervescent NASDAQ index, which had increased over 100 percent during the past year, also peaked. From that point on it literally was downhill: The bull market of the 1990s was over. By the end of 2000 the NASDQ index had declined over 50 percent, investors losing about $3 trillion in paper wealth. Although not as sharp, Figure 2.4 shows that the DJIA began a downward slide that did not end until 2003.

What "caused" the 2000 break? One candidate is monetary policy. As in earlier episodes, the Federal Reserve pushed interest rates higher during 1999. After dealing with the financial crises of 1998, the Federal Reserve embarked on a policy to quash any resurgence of inflation. To do this, the Fed increased the federal funds rate from about 4.5 percent in early 1999 to 6.5 percent by spring 2000.

Another "cause" sometimes suggested is the increased amount of insider selling that began in late 1999. Between September 1999 and July 2000, the value of insider stock sales, usually done in large blocks, rose to slightly more than $43 billion (Mahar, 2003). In fact, during the first six months of 2000 alone, insider block sales amounted to $39 billion, much more pronounced than for all of 1997–98. Did those dumping their own company's stocks know that a break in the market would expose inflated earnings? The exposure of corporate scandal and eventual collapse of companies like Enron and Global Crossing to name a couple, gave investors, especially institutional investors, reason enough to bail out. The market lost all the momentum of the previous years and even as the market drifted lower in 2001, the tragic events of September 11, 2001, pushed it down further: The DJIA, which was 11,722 in January 2000, was 8,920.7 when the market reopened on September 17, 2001. It took until 2006 for the DJIA to approach its pre-2000 level.

## SUMMARY

The market's development was transformed by several notable episodes of boom and bust. Using the four major market breaks of the twentieth century as a guide, the market survived each downfall, often gaining additional regulatory oversight. In 1907 this took the form of a central bank, the Federal Reserve, established in part to stabilize financial markets. The famous Crash of 1929 dramatically changed how the government regulates the securities market with the installment of new market and trading regulations. These changes were so significant that most form the foundation for current regulations. More recently, the 1987 crash led to regulators trying to figure out how to keep ahead of the technology of trading. Their answer was to institute circuit breakers that stop trading when the markets get too hectic. And after the recent 2000 downturn, the focus has been on corporate fraud as companies tried to artificially inflate earnings and, therefore, stock prices.

We barely scratched the surface of the stock market's history. As you might imagine, a detailed treatment would (and does) fill volumes. The foregoing provides a glimpse into the development of the U.S. stock market, from its humble beginnings in the late 1700s to the key institution that it is today. Not only has the market changed as new technologies came along, but it also changed as regulators sought to protect investors and establish orderly markets. In every case, the intention is to provide an avenue by which financial capital is efficiently distributed. As we will see in Chapter Seven, this is crucial to maintaining growth of the economy and the well-being of its citizens.

## NOTES

1. Robert Sobel, *The Big Board: A History of the New York Stock Market* (New York: Free Press, 1965), 20.

2. Ibid.

3. Richard J. Teweles and Edward S. Bradley, *The Stock Market*, 5th ed. (New York: John Wiley, 1987), 85.

4. Ibid.

5. Sobel, *The Big Board*, 81.

6. John Kenneth Galbraith, *The Great Crash: 1929* (Boston: Houghton Mifflin, 1955), 12.

7. Cited in Galbraith, *The Great Crash*, 20.

8. Ibid., 93.

9. Ibid., 43.

10. Ibid., 179.

11. Ibid., 365.

12. Ibid., 96.

13. Ibid., 115.

14. Maggie Mahar, *Bull: A History of the Boom, 1982–1999* (New York: HarperBusiness, 2003), 50.

15. Avner Arbel and Albert E. Kaff, *Crash: Ten Days in October . . . Will It Strike Again?* (New York: Longman, 1989), ix.

16. Tim Metz, *Black Monday: The Catastrophe of October 19, 1987 . . . and Beyond* (New York: William Morrow, 1988), 74.

17. Ibid., 88.

18. Ibid.

19. Robert T. Parry, "The October '87 Crash Ten Years Later," Federal Reserve Bank of San Francisco *Economic Letter* 96–332 (1997).

20. Cited in Mahar, *A History of the Boom*, 72.

21. Dale W. Jorgenson, "Information Technology and the U.S. Economy," *American Economic Review* 91, no. 1 (2001): 1–32, 1–2.

22. Robert Hall, "Struggling to Understand the Stock Market," *American Economic Review* 91, no. 2 (2001): 1–11, 1.

23. Cited in Mahar, *A History of the Boom*, 300.

24. Ibid.

25. Ibid., 272.

# Three

## Stocks in Today's Economy

Stocks are financial securities that represent claims of ownership. A stockholder is a partial owner of the firm: the stock represents the investor's "pro rata" or proportional ownership of the business. A share of stock gives the shareholder a right to a pro rata share of the business's profits or, in the case of liquidation, the pro rata right to the value of the business's assets in excess of its liabilities. There are two ways to view ownership rights. One as a going concern in which case the stockholder gets a pro rata share of profits and bears a pro rata share of losses. The second case occurs when the business is liquidating or selling itself off. In this case, the stockholder gets a pro rata share of any excess in the value of the assets over the liabilities that have been paid off. A share of common stock also gives the shareholder a right to vote in the election of the board of directors. It is the board of directors who take an active role in seeing that all shareholders' rights are recognized and maximized.

Stocks therefore can be viewed as a contractual arrangement between two parties, the party investing in the firm and the firm itself. The investor's willingness to give up money for the stock represents the expectation that they will receive some future payment that exceeds what they have given up. This expected gain cannot be exceeded elsewhere. On the other side, the firm needed the new funds coming from the investor when the stock was issued. It is willing to agree to turn over at least some of the ownership to the investor in order to acquire these funds. As such, stock is really a security that represents an ownership claim.

An important aspect of this claim to the investor is the protection offered by the corporate structure. Shareholders have limited liabilities; that is, the maximum that a stockholder can lose is his or her original investment. Should the corporation fail or be found negligent in some legal manner, shareholders cannot be called upon to put up more money than they originally invested in the corporation.

Because a common stock can be viewed from two different perspectives, that of the firm and that of the investor, it is useful to examine these more carefully. From the perspective of the firm, why does a firm obligate itself by issuing common stock? Also, what factors influence the size of the stock issuance? From the perspective of the investor, why would an investor give up funds for a pro rata claim on a business? We will examine the different means by which investors can gain from owning stock.

## STOCK AS A FUNDING SOURCE

Why would a business agree to give investors a claim against its future earnings? The answer is simply that the firm trades partial ownership in order to use the funds that it gets from the investor. When shares of stock are sold for the first time, this activity is referred to as an initial public offering (IPO). In such an offering newly created shares are being sold for the first time. As economies are growing and opportunities are being presented to exploit new technologies, businesses often need injections of funds in order to expand. Issuing stock has been a great source of funds for business growth and development.

### THE INITIAL PUBLIC OFFERING (IPO)

An initial public offering is the first time that the general public is given the opportunity to buy stock and invest in a firm. In addition to being a first offering, an IPO is a public offering. This means that anyone willing to pay the asked price for a share is given the right to buy a share of the stock. As a public offering an IPO must meet and satisfy certain requirements established by the Securities Exchange Commission (SEC). For example, possible share-holders must be given a prospectus that defines how the monies invested will be used and the risk that the investor is likely to face from their invest-ment.

A firm that offers stock in an IPO usually uses the services of an investment bank to make sure that the legal requirements are being met, and to make sure that the stock is properly priced. This latter function ensures such that there is sufficient investor demand for the offering so that all stock will be sold. An investment bank is, therefore, simply an intermediary: that is, a go-between for the firm issuing the stock and the investors buying the stock. Investment banks frequently have their own investor clients that they initially sell the IPO stock to. Since the firm is receiving the cash from the IPO, it is in the firm's best interest to see that the price it gets for a share of stock is the maximum possible. Interestingly, research about IPOs generally shows that IPOs are under-priced when first sold. This is indicated by the fact that many stocks generally appreciate a small amount on their first day of public trading. This finding suggests that one could make significant returns by buying stocks at their IPO and holding them.

## SECONDARY MARKET TRANSACTIONS

Most investors do not buy stock at their IPO but buy stock from another investor at some later date. These transactions are secondary market transaction. The key difference is that in the secondary market transaction, the firm for which the stock represents an ownership obligation receives nothing from the transaction. Unlike an IPO, a secondary market transaction simply represents an exchange between two investors. One investor is selling the stock that the other investor is buying. The only significance that this exchange has to the firm is that it is now notified that one of its shareholders has changed.

The vast majority of transactions involving stocks are secondary market transactions and not IPOs. The investor makeup is changing on a day-to-day basis in the U.S. financial system with more and more households owning stocks. It is becoming rarer, however, that a business is getting a new injection of funds. This means that as a source of funds for businesses in the United States, IPOs are relatively less important than, say, business loans from financial institutions, such as banks, or other financial sources like the commercial paper market.

When engaged in a secondary market transaction, investors use securities brokers and dealers to assist in the buying and selling of existing stock. In other words, an investor who wants to sell stock finds a broker or dealer to aid in finding someone to buy the stock. Similarly, the buyer of a stock uses a broker to help find the selling party. Sometimes a buyer uses a dealer who already owns the stock in their own portfolios. Only IPOs use the services of an investment bank. Buyers and sellers of existing securities use the service of brokers and dealers.

## SECONDARY OFFERINGS

Sometimes a business that already has raised funds through an IPO decides that it wants to issue more stock and raise additional funds. Perhaps it wishes to expand its product line or open new stores in other towns. In this case, the stock offering is referred to as a secondary offering, indicating that the firm has already offered stock once before. A secondary offering, therefore, is another source of new funds. However, because more stock is outstanding following secondary offering, the ownership of the business is spread more widely. It is in this sense that a secondary offering results in a "dilution of ownership." If the firm had ten shares outstanding and chose to issue an additional five shares in a secondary offering, each shareholder now has a claim to one-fifteenth of the firm compared with the original claim to one-tenth of the firm. Because of this effect, the original shareholders (owners) of the firm must approve secondary offerings. They would be willing to dilute their ownership if they believe the addition of new funds will expand the business and raise profits. If issuing more stock allows the firm to better succeed, the value of their one-fifteenth ownership is expected to exceed the value of their original ownership share.

### PRIVATE PLACEMENT VERSUS PUBLIC STOCK

Common stock is offered either through a private sell or a public auction. Private sells usually occur when the investors are known beforehand and are familiar with the managers of the firm. In the case of private sell, the securities do not have to adhere to as many of the SEC's rules and regulations. Because of this, it is generally less expensive to issue a private stock compared with a public stock.

Privately placed securities, after they have been first issued to investors, are more difficult to sell in the secondary market than publicly traded stocks. Because these securities are not publicly listed, the seller will not have the assistance of an exchange like the New York Stock Exchange (NYSE) in aiding the sale. Due to this feature, privately placed stocks are perceived as being much harder to exchange—less liquid—than publicly traded stocks. There is less certainty what the seller is willing to offer for the stock in the secondary transaction.

Because of the potential liquidity problems with private stock, many firms find it worthwhile to go through the process of listing their securities on a public exchange and registering them with the SEC. Indeed, any corporation that has more than 500 shareholders is required to register its securities with the SEC. In this case, the stocks are public stocks and they generally trade on formal exchanges. Prices of publicly traded stocks generally are widely available and the transaction costs of buying or selling public stocks are generally lower than for private stocks.

In this day and age, investors generally focus on publicly traded stocks. Given the size and importance of the major stock exchanges in the United States—for instance, the NYSE or the AMEX—most discussion of the stock market focuses on publicly traded stocks. For example, often-heard measures of the market value of stock (calculated as the market price of each share times the number of shares outstanding and summed for all stocks in that particular market) are based on stocks traded on the major exchanges. Still, there are many private stock securities in the U.S. financial system that provide financial capital to smaller businesses. Moreover, even some large corporations in the United States choose to remain private. There are two advantages commonly cited for remaining private as opposed to going public. First, as long as a corporation has less than 500 shareholders it does not have to register with the SEC. This means that the corporation can save on the large expenses associated with such registration. In addition to saving registration fees, private corporations today are not required to follow the new Sarbanes-Oxley laws regarding public disclosure of financial information. Third, many private corporations today laud the fact that their shareholders are not worried about quarter to quarter changes in the firms' financial performance. Rather, private equity shareholders, since they have difficulty selling their investments, are generally felt to have a longer-term perspective regarding the corporation.

## COMMON STOCK VERSUS PREFERRED STOCK

Stock is a term used broadly to refer to a security that represents ownership of a business. There are two different types of such securities. The most common type is called common stock. Common stock is a security that does not promise any payments, which are called dividends. While common stocks frequently pay dividends (many times on a quarterly basis or at least annually) it is important to understand that the business is not *obligated* to make such payments. Indeed, the business can only make dividend payments if all other obligations are paid first. Preferred stock is different than common stock, because the firm states a dividend payout rate as an obligation. Owners of preferred stock generally expect fixed payments coming from the business (dividends). These owners also must be paid prior to any common stock dividend payments.

Individual investors in the United States generally do not own much preferred stock due to a special tax feature of preferred stock. Any corporation that owns preferred stock in another corporation pays taxes on 15 percent of the dividend payment. Individuals who are preferred stockholders do not enjoy this same advantage, however. Individuals pay taxes on the full dividend payment. Because preferred stock has this tax advantage for corporations, most preferred stock in the United States is held by other corporations and not by individual investors. For this reason common stock is much more prevalent in the U.S. financial system than preferred stock.

### STOCK VERSUS BONDS

Owning a stock is an agreement between an investor and a business that is very different from the agreement provided to bondholders. Bondholders are not owners of the business; they are debt holders. The business agrees to be obligated to—indebts itself—bondholders in exchange for receiving funds. Most bonds offer periodic payments, generally semi-annual, that are called coupon payments. Coupon payments are obligations of the business and not making them in the time promised is grounds for entering bankruptcy proceedings. Unlike stocks, bonds generally have a fixed maturity date that reflects the date of the last payment, which includes the last coupon payment and the principal that the business initially borrowed.

So, while bonds represent another source of funds for businesses, there are important differences between stocks and bonds. Most importantly, the business is obligated make all necessary payments to bondholders prior to making any payments to stockholders, including those who own preferred stock. Also, bonds generally have a fixed maturity, indicating that the full amount borrowed is to be paid back at a certain future date. Stock, on

Stocks can be traded in all types of industries—from commodities like coffee to heavy industry, high-tech, and pharmaceuticals. Photo courtesy of Getty Images/ PhotoLink.

the other hand, has no maturity date because it represents continuous ownership.

## STOCKS AS AN INVESTMENT

A stock is an agreement between a firm and a shareholder who claims some pro rata ownership of the firm. The firm agrees to this arrangement as a means of getting new funds to use for expansion or to pay off some of its existing obligations. The investor parts with their funds because they anticipate to be compensated by way of economic gain from their ownership. The compensation given to stockholders is generally referred to as a return.

Stockholders realize economic gain in two different forms. First, a profitable business can pay out profits in the form of dividends, even though they are not required to do so. Most large, well-known corporations make it a common practice to pay dividends on a regular basis and increase the amount of dividends paid to shareholders when business is good. Second, investors gain when the value of their stock appreciates. This is referred to as a capital gain. If a corporation makes a profit but does not pay it out in the form of a dividend, then the firm will retain these earnings and the pro rata value of each shareholder's ownership increases in value. In the case of publicly traded stocks, this would show up as rising stock prices. Why? Because more investors bid up the stock's price since the firm is now worth more.

### Dividends and Capital Gains

Large corporations in the United States on average pay out less than one-half of their profits in the form of dividends; they keep the other half in the form of retained earnings. The practice of paying out dividends can vary greatly from one firm to another, however. For example, Berkshire Hathaway, the large corporation run by Warren Buffet, one of the wealthiest individuals in the country, has made it a practice of not paying out dividends at all. Shareholders of Berkshire Hathaway stock have received no periodic payments in the form of dividends over time. They have, however, seen significant appreciation in the value of their stock as the corporation plowed profits back into the firm for new business investments. At the other extreme, most utilities pay out a fairly large share of their profits to shareholders as dividends. Their investors often count on the periodic dividend payments, much the same way that bondholders count on the periodic coupon payments.

As just described, shareholders can count on gains in one of two ways. Firms differ as to which strategy they choose to reward shareholders. Because of this, many professionals believe that stockholders fall into two groups in their decisions on where to invest. One group favors investment returns in the form of periodic dividend payments. Because these payments occur in a generally predictable fashion, it is like receiving income from the firm. Thus, stocks that favor dividends to reward shareholders generally are referred to as income stocks. Retirees counting on periodic cash flows from dividends represent investors who prefer income stocks. Utility companies, such as your local electric company, generally are income stocks. Also, preferred stock generally is considered a good income stock since its dividends generally are high and must be paid out prior to dividends on common stock.

Some investors do not need the predictable cash flows and are quite comfortable in letting the firm retain the profits to enhance future returns. Indeed, some investors prefer such an investment vehicle since this minimizes their tax obligations. As long as the investor retains their shares, their unrealized gains come with no tax obligation, unlike dividends that require the stockholder to claim the return on their annual income tax. Stocks that do not pay dividends but reward their shareholders with gain in the form of capital appreciation generally are referred to as capital appreciation or growth stocks. Berkshire Hathaway is a classic example of a capital appreciation stock: it pays no dividend and the price of each share has (and is expected to) increased over time.

Of course, some firms find it advantageous to change how they compensate investors. Microsoft is a good example. For years, Microsoft, as a public corporation, paid out no dividends at all, like Berkshire Hathaway. The firm found it could put its profits to good use internally, and their investors showed no evidence that dividends were important to them. However, with recent tax law changes that resulted in dividends being taxed only at a 15 percent rate, Microsoft felt it was better to return monies to the shareholders in the form of dividends. Shareholders who thought they owned a capital appreciation/growth stock found themselves with sizeable dividends (and tax bills) coming to them. But, given the relatively low tax rate that they had to pay on the dividends, shareholders probably were not too upset. Some financial observers see this change as Microsoft sending a signal to financial markets that they do not see the good internal investment opportunities that they once predicted.

## STOCK RETURNS

It is important to remember that stockholders can receive economic gain in one of two forms. Too frequently, investors focus on the predictable and timely dividend payments to the exclusion of considering capital appreciation. However, the example of Berkshire Hathaway, which has not paid any dividends at all but has rewarded investors with quite sizeable capital appreciation, is a good one to bear in mind. Investors who did not need the steady cash flow from dividends and kept their money invested in Berkshire Hathaway have been rewarded over time with sizeable stock returns.

The best measure of what stockholders gain from their investment is called total return or stock return. The stock return is the sum of all gains from the investment (dividend plus capital appreciation) divided by the amount originally invested. For example, suppose someone bought 100 shares of stock in Hancock Bank for $37.00 a share one year ago. Suppose further that today the shares are trading at $39.53. Now assume this investor received a total of $40.45 in dividend payments last year. Over the last year, the total is $253 in capital gain ($3,953.00 minus $3,700.00, and $40.45 from dividends paid out. Dividing the total dollar gain of $293.45 by the original investment of $3,700 gives a return of 0.0793, or 7.93%. Calculated on an annual basis as in this example, this return can be compared to interest rates quoted on bank deposits (such as CDs) and bonds to see how wise the stock purchase was.

RISK-RETURN TRADE-OFF

Common stock promises shareholders nothing explicitly: common stock-holders are residual claimants and only get what is left after claims by bondholders and preferred stockholders are satisfied. This is very different than a deposit at a bank, which promises investors a fixed return on their monies, or a bond that promises fixed periodic payments. Since common stock does not promise shareholders any explicit compensation, it is viewed as a relatively risky investment. The risk is that the investor is not certain what they will get back for their investment. If the company does well and is profitable, the common stockholder will be compensated. On the other hand, if profits are small or if the firm loses money, the shareholder can lose out on their investment. When profits are small, the amount paid out in dividends and/or retained in earnings will be small. Regardless, the investor is likely to be disappointed with their investment return. Of course, there is very little downside protection and the investor may lose everything. This generally occurs when a business is forced into bankruptcy and finds that the value of their outstanding liabilities exceeds the value of what the firm owns. Common stockholders in a firm that fails receive nothing on their investment.

Given this possibility, why would anyone risk losing everything they have invested? Would not it be better to invest in something like a bank deposit or a bond where the investor knows that they will get something back on their investment? With hindsight someone who loses all their investment of course would prefer something that gave them a return, no matter how small. But hindsight does not work for the investor facing the decision today of how best to use their money. The reason that investors choose to own stock, even if it is risky as an investment, is that they expect to be compensated for bearing the risk. Indeed, history and experience normally show that investors generally are compensated for bearing the risk of loss. Investors in common stock in the United States have realized returns that exceed those on most alternative investments, especially depositing money in a bank or buying bonds either issued by the government or corporations. In other words, investors expect to be compensated with higher returns for bearing the risk of investing in common stock.

Note that this comparison uses a large sample of common stocks as a basis of comparison. The large sample tells us that if an investor owns a diversified portfolio that is, a combination of many companies' stock), they would have received better gains than from the alternative investments. This does not mean, however, that all stock investors have gained more than they could have from alternatives. Indeed, recent history is full of corporations that have failed, meaning that investors lose everything invested in that company. For example, Enron and WorldCom are instances of investors losing all their invested funds due to corporate failure.

### Portfolios and Risk

A basic principle in finance is that investors can reduce their overall financial risk by investing in a number of different corporations instead of putting all their money in one business. By doing so, the investor attempts to offset losses in one or two companies' stocks with gains in the other stocks owned. Diversifying one's investment portfolio puts the "law of large numbers" (basically, it is easier to predict the average of a large group than to predict one individual occurrence) to work. Investors do not have to worry about one isolated case of loss (owning Enron), and can have greater confidence in predicting their stock return.

Investing a fixed amount of money in just one stock is riskier than investing the same amount in ten to twenty different stocks. Since it really is not that much more expensive to invest in a number of stocks versus just one (one can invest in a stock index fund, for example), basic finance models presume that investors generally purchase a broad portfolio of common stocks. This means investing in just one stock as opposed to ten increases the risk of loss. But, since this risk can be avoided fairly cheaply, the compensation for bearing this risk is reduced. This is one of the rare instances in finance that risk does not appear to be rewarded. An investment in a diversified portfolio of

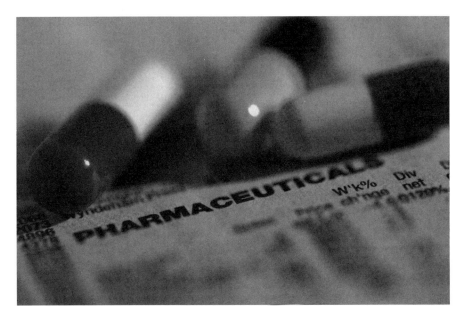

Stocks are traded in the pharmaceutical industry. Photo courtesy of Corbis.

common stock is still more risky than an investment in bonds, but investors can expect to earn a higher return. There is no easy way to avoid this risk, so investors are compensated for bearing it.

## RISK OVER TIME

Investors not only face risk that differs from one stock to another (some stocks are riskier than others), but investors also face risk that changes over time. In certain time periods called bull markets, it is generally found that most stocks increase in value and that stock returns on most stocks yield a higher return than their historical averages. Investors who own a diversified portfolio of stocks are generally happy investors in bull markets. On the other hand, sometimes it appears that most stock prices decline in value and stock returns are abnormally low and even negative. In such markets, referred to as bear markets, investors can lose money even with a well-diversified portfolio.

After the fact, it is fairly easy to identify whether a period coincides with a bull or a bear market by comparing returns with historical norms. The Great Depression that followed the Crash of 1929 encompassed a bear market as most investors lost substantial amounts of their investments in the stock market. It often, though mistakenly, is believed that the 1929 stock market crash caused the Great Depression. Although a contributing factor, the crash was not the sole cause of the Great Depression. More recently, the "bubble" correction that began in 2000 represents another bear market in which investors lost substantial paper wealth from their investments in stocks.

The mid-1980s and most of the 1990s, on the other hand, are considered bull markets. Investments in diversified portfolios of U.S. stock during these times resulted in not only positive stock returns, but returns that were far higher than historical averages.

One of the interesting observations about investing in stocks in the United States is that not only diversification helps smooth out returns and lowers risk, but time also seems to do a similar thing. This is one of the main themes of Jeremy Siegel's 2002 book *Stocks for the Long Run*. After examining 200 years of financial market return data for the United States, he points out that there has never been a thirty-year period in the United States in which stocks have yielded lower returns than bonds.[1] This statement includes the Great Depression as a part of the sample, in which investors in stocks lost fortunes. History tells us that if these stockholders could have stuck with a diversified stock portfolio through the substantial losses in the early 1930s, over time

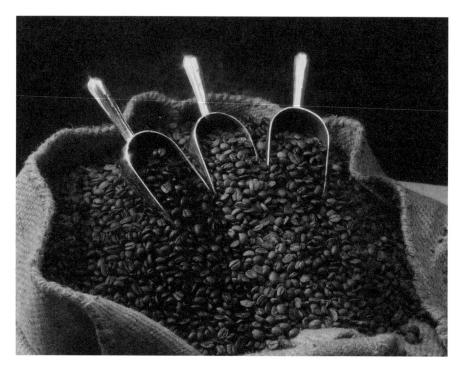

The coffee industry is a traded stock. Photo courtesy of Getty Images/Greg Kuchik.

they would have been rewarded with returns that far exceeded those of investing in safer securities like bonds.

The record on stock market performance calls attention to the fact that stock investors should never forget their two allies: diversification and time. Patient investors who diversify their stocks across many different industries and sizes of corporations, and who hold their investment for many years, are rewarded with positive returns that exceed the alternatives that appear safer on the surface. This result should not be too surprising, though. Stocks are risky investments and investors must be compensated for bearing this risk. The historical record indicates that patient investors have been rewarded with high returns for bearing this risk. These investors provide the wherewithal for businesses, both start-ups and large mature corporations, to search for new profit opportunities both in the United States and the world economy.

## BASIC INVESTMENT STRATEGIES

Investors in the stock market and other investment vehicles often use different strategies. For example, the passive buy and hold strategy is one approach. An investor selects a diversified portfolio of stocks, invests in each, and then reinvests dividends and gains over many years. It is the strategy that Jeremy Siegel's investigation suggests has much merit to it. As an alternative, some investors prefer to try and time the market. This requires an investor to invest fully in bull markets and to be out of stocks in bear markets. On the surface, it would appear that market timers would do much better in maximizing their investment gains, especially given the short-term volatility described above. Surely, being out of the market when stock prices are falling and being in the market when they are rising, yields greater returns than the buy and hold strategy.

While it is obvious that being able to time the market would result in substantial gains, it is very difficult to correctly identify changes in the investment climate. As an example, would you say that we are currently in a bull market or a bear market? For most investors, this is a very difficult question to answer. If we cannot properly identify the current climate, how can we successfully decide when to be in the market and when to be out of the market? Academic studies into the ability to time the market find very little evidence that anyone can successfully do this on a consistent basis. For instance, mutual funds pay professional managers large sums of money to make such decisions and the evidence suggests that they are not any more successful (in terms of total returns) than employing the simple buy and hold strategy.

One other aspect of timing makes it more difficult to use as a successful investment strategy. Because any one day can result in huge moves in stock prices and returns, market timers must be able to identify broad trends but also to identify specific days when those trends change. Another way of stating this is to note that the strong positive returns that stocks have achieved over extended periods of time actually occur on just a few days. For example, Siegel estimates that from 1982 to 1999, stocks had a total return of 17.3 percent.[2] This return was accomplished by being in stocks everyday and reinvesting dividends back into the market. However, for those investors who made the wrong decision about being in the market on only twenty-four days during this period, their returns were cut by one-third. This is because these two dozen days experienced the largest percentage point gains over this period. In other words, even if the investor properly identified the period as a good bull market, and if they had been trying to time the market on just a few days over the whole period but did not properly identify those few days, they would have experienced much lower return than a buy-and-hold investor. In this sense, it is important to understand that investing in the stock market for the long haul means being in the market on a daily basis. In summary, there is very little evidence to support the notion of market timing as a good, consistent investment strategy.

## Large Cap versus Small Cap

Another investment strategy relates to the size of the corporations to invest in. This approach centers on the market capitalization of the corporation; that is, the market value of common stock outstanding for a firm. Market capitalization is measured by taking the number of shares that a firm has outstanding multiplied it by the share price. The Dow Jones Industrial Average (DJIA), for example, monitors the stock prices of thirty particular "large cap" firms. The names of these firms are familiar, including American Express, General Electric, Microsoft, Intel, and Wal-Mart. Large cap corporations extend beyond the thirty blue-chip companies in the DJIA. The 500 companies that comprise the Standard and Poor's 500 (S&P 500) Index also are generally considered large cap stocks. Beyond the largest 500 or so companies in the United States, the next tier is labeled mid-cap stocks. These are not the largest, or the smallest firms in terms of market capitalization. The other group comprises small cap stocks, publicly traded corporations with the lowest market capitalization in the United States.

Two alternative investment strategies recommend investing at either of the two extremes in terms of market capitalization. One strategy favors buying small cap stocks, the other favors large cap stocks. There are obvious grounds for each position. Small cap companies are likely to be the current innovators in the economy. They represent new products or services or delivery vehicles for each. And it is important to recognize that many of today's large cap stocks were small cap stocks just a few years ago. Witness the evolution of Microsoft, Hewlett-Packard, and Dell just to name a few. Corporations that are large cap firms today may have started in garages and university dorm rooms just a few years ago. Those who invested with these firms when they first issued stock have all been rewarded handsomely for their investments (and risk taking).

The obvious downside for small cap stocks is the fact that they are not well known. Investors thus have more limited information available when making informed investment decisions. Moreover, it is well known that many small start-up firms do not survive. For every Microsoft success, there are many small start-up firms that fail. But do not take this to mean that only small firms fail. Recently, a number of large cap corporations failed, including several major airlines, Enron, and WorldCom just to name a few. But large cap stocks generally have longer histories of business success and more financial market analysts looking closely over the shoulders of these companies

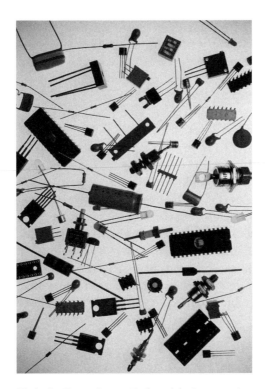

Today's Dow Jones Industrial Average includes several computer and telecommunications firms. Photo courtesy of Corbis.

than for small cap companies. Indeed, it frequently is the case that very few financial market analysts are watching over the small cap corporations.

While a case then can be made for investing in small cap firms or large cap firms, the evidence found in academic and practitioner studies generally supports the view that returns are slightly higher for the small cap firms. Still, this difference in investment performance is small in magnitude and it is widely known that it does not always hold up. For instance, some say the superior performance of small cap stocks is driven by a short period of time in the early 1980s. Since the 1990s witnessed large cap stocks doing better than small cap stocks, there probably is little to recommend one strategy over the other. Rather, it is probably wise to diversify, owning some large and small cap stocks, as well as middle size or mid-cap group.

### GROWTH VERSUS VALUE

Another contrast in investing styles is the growth as opposed to value strategies. Growth strategies focus on investing in companies that have the greatest potential for gaining higher earnings in the future. Here, the issue of what the stock is currently selling for is not the focal point. Rather, attention turns to finding those companies that have the greatest potential for improving profitability in the future. In addition, the fact that a company is or is not paying out much in the way of dividends also is not that important to a growth investor. A growth strategy is to find such companies and buy their stock with the expectation that they will experience substantial increases in their stock price over time. A good starting place is to look at recent earnings, in particular, comparing today's earnings to the recent past. To be identified as a growth stock, one would need to see substantial increases in the company's earnings, along with the expectation that such earnings growth will continue in the foreseeable future.

Value investment strategies, in contrast, focus first and foremost on the current price of the stock. This strategy seeks to find stocks that are "cheap" with the expectation that the company will soon realize its full potential and their stock price will appreciate. In addition to analyzing the current stock price, a value strategy emphasizes the dividends that a business pays out. Indeed, one thing that makes a particular stock appear cheap is sizeable dividend payouts. The value approach to investing considers growth opportunities as relatively unimportant, at least relative to the current price and payout record.

Many times these two investment strategies are characterized as substitutes. You might ask yourself which of these strategies has been most successful in the past. In such a comparison, there is no universal winner. In certain periods, the growth strategy seems to yield the highest returns, while in other periods, the value strategy yields the highest returns. Still, over the longest period available, the evidence tends to support the value approach, albeit by a small margin.

## SUMMARY

Stocks play an ever increasing role in almost everyone's lives in a market economy such as the United States. Stocks represent an invaluable source of funding for many new start-up businesses. Without such funds, it is likely that the substantial business and technological advances seen in the past would not have occurred. Stockholders bear the risk that a business will not survive. Without investors taking this risk, many opportunities for business advancement probably would have remained on the designer's table. The historical record indicates that not all stockholders were rewarded for bearing this risk. Some have staked ownership claims in enterprises that failed, many times losing all their initial investment. However, investors who invest in a number of different firms and willingly hold those investments for many years appear to be rewarded for bearing the risk. Indeed, the returns on such an investment strategy generally exceed the safer investments such as buying bonds or investing funds into safe but low-return bank deposits.

## NOTES

1. Jeremy J. Siegel, *Stocks for the Long Run: The Definitive Guide to Financial Market Returns and Long-Term Investment Strategies*, 3rd ed. (New York: McGraw-Hill, 2002).

2. Ibid.

# Four

# Today's Stock Market in Action

This chapter starts by recognizing that when someone talks about trading stocks, they are generally referring to those shares bought and sold on a major stock exchange like the New York Stock Exchange (NYSE). However, not all stocks are publicly traded: Some stocks are not listed on any exchange but still are traded. We will examine that difference first. This chapter also provides a brief background on the major stock exchanges in the United States, where publicly traded stocks are bought and sold. It does not cover the history of the exchanges, but focuses on their role in the financial marketplace. The major stock indexes discussed throughout this book and used to measure the performance of the stock market or certain sectors of the market are covered, too. A key concept that helps explain market behavior, the notion of "market efficiency," is explored, covering both the pros and cons of this idea. Finally, we look into some of the different ways in which stock analysis is done, focusing on the fundamental and technical forms.

## PRIVATE VERSUS PUBLICLY TRADED STOCKS

Most stocks in the United States are traded on one of the major exchanges. It is important to recognize that not all stocks held or exchanged in the United States are publicly traded, however. Many smaller corporations (S corporations, for example) do not list their stocks on an exchange. A key difference in the different types of corporations relates to the tax treatment. Unlike the more recognized C corporations, smaller S corporations generally do not pay taxes as an entity, but pass profits on to shareholders who pay taxes at the individual level. Another difference is that S corporations must have less than 100 shareholders. This restriction alone explains why most S corporation stock is not publicly traded.

Transactions dealing with such stocks are referred to as private. Investors who own privately traded stock can sell their stock to others, just like owners of publicly traded stock. A key difference is that such transactions are not regulated by the government. An exchange of private stock means that the parties selling the stock and those buying the stock simply come to an agreement to trade at some price. Private stocks generally do not trade regularly. This means that transactions in such stocks may take more time to execute than publicly traded stocks. The reason is because there often is less information available about the business and so more uncertainty (less publicly available information) about the underlying value of the stock. In the world of finance, it is said that a private stock is less "liquid" than a public stock. Even though trading in private stock differs from public stock in certain respects, possessing a share of a private stock still represents residual ownership of the firm as discussed in chapter three.

As you might expect, publicly traded stocks generally are those of the largest corporations in the United States. Even though there are more S corporations in theUnited States than C corporations, this numerical difference overstates the economic significance of small private stock ownership. Much more of the overall wealth in U.S. corporations is in publicly traded entities than in private stock. At the same time, one should not ignore the importance of stock ownership in small businesses such as S corporations.

## STOCK EXCHANGES

Publicly traded stocks are bought and sold on exchanges. The oldest stock exchange in the United States is the NYSE where members have been buying and selling stock since 1792. (See Chapter Two for more detail.) The NYSE was first incorporated as a not-for-profit status in 1971 and in 2006 changed to a for-profit status when it merged with Archipelago. This means that shares of the NYSE are now publicly traded, just like that of General Electric or Ford. Most stocks exchanged on the NYSE are bought and sold through members of the exchange from the major brokerage houses. Many exchange members serve as market makers on the floor, taking the opposite side of buy and sell orders as they arrive.

Today, the NYSE lists the stocks of about 2,800 corporations. To be listed on the NYSE a corporation must meet certain standards in terms of the value of the stock outstanding and trading volume, amongst many other considerations. In addition, firms must pay a fee to be listed on the NYSE. Each and every stock that you may wish to buy is not listed on the NYSE. For example,

Google stock is not listed on the NYSE. Still, the NYSE lists the stocks of most major corporations, just not all.

There are two other major national exchanges, plus numerous regional exchanges operating in the United States. In addition to the NYSE, some stocks are traded on the National Association of Securities Dealers Automated Quotation (NASDAQ) exchange, others on the American Stock Exchange (AMEX).

The NASDAQ exchange is unlike the NYSE in that it is an electronic exchange. That is, there is no floor upon which traders meet face-to-face to trade stocks. Trading on the NASDAQ exchange is done over an electronic network between brokers. In fact, the NASDAQ market is the world's largest electronic exchange. Another key difference between these two exchanges is that each one has different listing requirements. This means that corporations must meet different rules before their stocks can be bought and sold on each exchange. Because of this, each exchange trades a mostly different set of stocks, although a few companies are listed on both of these major exchanges. For instance, companies listed on the NASDAQ exchange generally are relatively newer companies than those listed on the NYSE. Also, NASDAQ listing boasts a higher proportion of technology-related companies relative to the NYSE. Investors can also buy ownership of the NASDAQ exchange by buying its stock which is listed on the NASDAQ.

The other national exchange is the AMEX. Today, the AMEX is not nearly as large or important as the NYSE or the NASDAQ markets when it comes to the trading of stocks in the United States. Even so, the AMEX has gained a reputation for listing many of the newer instruments traded (e.g., derivative instruments and options).

## STOCK INDEXES

For many years investors have made use of stock indexes to track the general trends in stock prices. The three most popular U.S. stock indexes are the Dow Jones Industrial Average (DJIA), the S&P 500 index, and the NASDAQ composite index.

### Dow Jones Industrial Average

The oldest and best-known stock index in the United States is the DJIA, frequently referred to as simply the "Dow." While it is the most widely known stock index, it also is amongst the narrowest major market indexes. Indeed, the DJIA tracks only thirty individual stocks. While it is limited in the number of firms included, they are generally the largest and most widely traded stocks traded in the United States. They are the so-called blue-chip stocks. The Appendix lists changes in firms included in the DJIA over time.

The DJIA itself is compiled by combining the prices of the thirty stock prices that make up the index. The level of the index means little in and of itself. Rather, what is important to an investor is how the index changes over time. The change of the index, not its level, provides valuable information about the stock market and the total return to one's investment. For example, the news at night frequently reports how much the DJIA changed today relative to yesterday. Suppose it is reported that the "Dow" rose 120 points today. How should this be interpreted?

First, it means that the thirty stocks that make up the DJIA rose, on average, in price. Second, it means that if an investor owned this collection of stocks, they realized a positive gain for the day. This gain often is expressed as a percent of the index level. To illustrate, if the index closed yesterday at 11,000, today's close of 11,120 means that the average stock price in the index rose about one percent ($= 120/11,000$). Such a daily increase in the DJIA is not that unusual. There are times, gratefully few and far between, when the index falls sharply. On October 19, 1987, for instance, the DJIA dropped by about 19 percent, one of the largest percentage point declines in the stock market's history.

While the DJIA is the most popular stock index in the United States, it might be the least representative of the overall market. Not only does it cover only a handful of all the corporations, but it is also a specific kind of index: It is a price-weighted stock index. In other words, in constructing the DJIA, the largest weight is given to the company that has the highest stock price. There is no reason, however, to think that the company with the highest stock price is more important than any of the other stocks in the index. It may not even be the largest company.

To understand this, consider Berkshire Hathaway, which is not in the DJIA. This company does not pay out dividends, but retains substantial earnings that are used to build greater value. It also has not split. Many companies split their stocks when the price gets well above $100 per share. In the case of a two for one stock split, the owner of one share of stock prior to the split is given another share. This action does not affect the underlying value of the corporation, so the stock price should fall by one-half on the split. Berkshire Hathaway does neither.

What if this company was included in the DJIA? Berkshire Hathaway's stock recently (2006) traded at a price in excess of $80,000 per share. If Berkshire Hathaway's stock was in the DJIA, it would have a weight of at least 800 times the other stocks in the index. This is because the other stocks in the index have prices generally less than $100 per share. This example illustrates a problem with a price-weighted index. Even so, the advantages of the DJIA are that it is popular, easily understood, and has a long history.

## THE S&P 500

Probably the second most popular index in the United States is the S&P 500 index, constructed by the company Standard and Poor's. As the name suggests, this index is comprised of 500 stock prices, generally the larger corporations. In the case of the S&P 500, all prices are weighted by the company's market valuation. A company's market value is found by multiplying the price per share times the number of shares outstanding. This measure often is used to gauge the size of a corporation. For example, it was often commented on that General Motors was the largest corporation in the United States. This was based on the fact that its market value—share price multiplied by outstanding shares—exceeded that of any other corporation. Today, claim to being one of the largest corporations in the United States, based on market capitalization, is made by ExxonMobile, General Electric, and Microsoft. Although it is the largest retailer based on sales, Wal-Mart is not in the top five based on market capitalization. The greater the market value, the greater weight given that company's stock in the S&P 500 index.

Like the DJIA, the level of the S&P 500 index really does not provide much information by itself. Rather, as the index moves over time, changes in the level of the index are informative. In particular, the percentage change of the index—found by taking today's index value minus the value at an earlier date divided by the level of the index at the earlier date—provides a gauge of stock returns. This is what an investor is concerned about, the return from holding stock, not its level. The only time the level of the index is widely discussed is when the index reaches some all-time high.

## THE NASDAQ

Another popular index in the United States comes from the NASDAQ exchange, generally thought to represent the technology sector of the economy. There are two separate NASDAQ indexes that investors follow. One is the composite, which tracks all stock prices traded on the NASDAQ exchange. The other NASDAQ index tracks stock price movements of the 100 largest corporations traded on the NASDAQ exchange. Since NASDAQ stock prices generally are more volatile, these indexes have demonstrated greater volatility than either the DJIA or the S&P 500. For example, in early 2000 the NASDAQ composite index lost much more of its prepeak value than the DJIA or S&P 500. Indeed, by 2006, the NASDAQ composite remained far

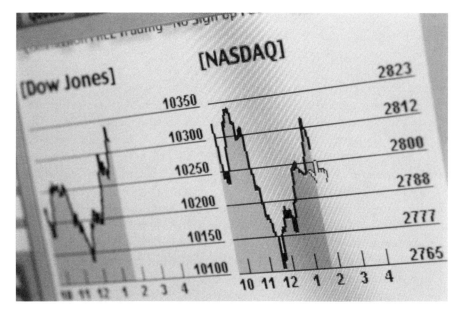

The Dow Jones Industrial Average and NASDAQ: benchmarks of trading activity.
Photo courtesy of Corbis.

below its peak value reached in early 2000. At the same time by mid-2006 the
DJIA was approaching its 2000 peak value.

### OTHER INDEXES

The Russell and the Wilshire indexes, like the S&P 500, track the stock
prices of a wide variety of companies. These indexes include many smaller
corporations not found in the others. Based on their market capitalization,
these smaller corporations are referred to as mid-cap firms and, for the
smallest publicly traded firms, small-cap. The Russell indexes generally are
used to track the performance of small and mid-cap firms. The Wilshire index
is the broadest major index, including stock prices of about 5,000 corporations. Both indexes are market value weighted, so larger firms are given more
weight in the index.

In addition to the major stock indexes in the United States, most countries
throughout the world have indexes to measure the performance of stock
prices in their countries. The FTSE 100, for example, measures stock prices
for 100 companies traded on the London Stock Exchange. The Nikkei 225
index similarly measures stock prices for companies listed on the Tokyo
exchange. (See Chapter Seven for discussion of major foreign indexes.)

All major developed countries have their own respective stock indexes. Today, even developing countries like Malaysia, Thailand, Brazil, Russia, India, and China have stock exchanges with stock indexes that change with the market's expectations of the profitability of the issuing corporations. There are even proprietary (available for a fee) indexes like those offered by Morgan Stanley that track stock prices for many different countries in the same index.

## EFFICIENT MARKETS

It often is difficult to gauge the performance of the stock market. For example, one day there is good news about the economy, say the unemployment rate falls by one percentage point. The nightly news says the stock market rallied on the announcement, pushing stock prices up. A month later the stock market might fall following similar economic news. This behavior may suggest to you that the stock market is quite fickle: It just can not seem to make up its mind.

There is a perfectly good explanation for this apparently erratic behavior. The explanation is based on the idea of efficient markets. While there is some debate concerning its validity, it remains a useful starting point to explain observed movements in stock prices.

To understand the idea of efficient markets, remember that stocks represent an ownership claim on the future profits of a firm. Investors are concerned about the future, not the past, in setting the value of a stock today. The past is only relevant to the extent it helps shape expectations for the future. The theory of efficient markets, therefore, is based on the idea that today's stock price reflects investors' expectations regarding the future. Their expectations are efficient in the sense that they reflect currently available information, such as the projected earnings of a firm. In other words, a rational investor would not intentionally ignore any relevant piece of information in forming their expectation if doing so could reduce the potential return on their investment. Consequently, the idea of efficient stock markets implies that "stock prices reflect all available information." If true, then the only thing that would cause a stock price to change is the arrival of new (unexpected) information.

Knowing what new information ("news") is being released usually is not sufficient to understand how the market will respond. To explain stock price movements, we not only should be concerned with the news but also on how that news relates to what investors expected. Let us return to the example of when the stock market rises when a decline in the unemployment rate is announced and the next time the stock market falls on the same announcement.

To explain this, we need to ask what investors expected the change in the unemployment rate to be in both instances.

Suppose that prior to the first announcement market participants expected no change in the unemployment rate. Then the news to financial market participants was that the economy was doing better than expected. This may translate into greater expected future earnings and stock prices rise. Suppose, however, that prior to the second announcement, investors expected the unemployment rate to fall. If the announced decline is more than expected, the news to financial market participants is that the economy may be weaker than anticipated. This may generate revised expectations of future earnings, and stock prices fall.

What the government told everyone about the economy was the same in both instances but the announced change in the unemployment rate was different from what the market expected. Viewed in this light, it is only natural to expect the stock market to behave differently even though the same information was provided.

## The Role of Expectations

The efficient markets view highlights the importance of expectations in explaining stock price changes over time. The basic principle is that what is expected by market participants is largely embedded in current stock prices. For example, if everyone expects that a company will announce very strong earnings for the next year, market participants act upon what is expected and price this into the current stock price. If the company then announces strong earnings, as expected, the efficient market hypothesis predicts that the stock price will not change when the earnings are announced. If the actual announcement is that earnings actually are expected to drop, this bit of contrary news will cause the stock's price to fall. Since the announcement went against the market's expectation, the new information caused the price to react. What happened was not as expected and the stock price adjusted to the new expectation.

To fully understand stock markets, we should always be asking ourselves what is expected, because the market's expectation is driving observed market prices. This is why the financial press is full of survey information, such as analysts' forecasts of future company earnings or economists' forecasts of the unemployment rate and inflation. Stock prices are constantly adjusting as expectations are changing. Besides, not everyone takes the same piece of information and comes up with the same expectation. This difference is what creates buyers and sellers. To keep up with the stock market, we should always be asking ourselves "what is priced into the market?" Knowing what is expected is never easy, but at least our attention is focused in the right direction.

China offers a good case study. The Chinese economy has been growing quite rapidly as the Chinese government has slowly allowed more and more of the economy to become market-oriented. The growth rate of the Chinese economy in the early 2000s is as much as three times that of other developed countries in the world. The naïve investor might say that China obviously is a great place to invest because this rapid economic growth will translate into healthy earnings growth. A student of market efficiency would be more cautious, wondering what market participants expect. If market participants expect a continuation of the strong economic growth experienced in recent years, current stock prices already reflect this. In this case, if China grows as expected, investors buying into the market today should not anticipate excessive total returns.

Remembering the idea of stock market efficiency might save a little time and agony the next time a broker calls with a great stock tip. Ask the broker why this information, if they already know it, is not priced into the firm's current stock price. If the broker does not have a good answer, they are probably just trying to sell something and not looking out for your best financial interests. Unless you are convinced that the broker really knows something that is not priced into the market, there is little reason to expect high returns based on such a tip.

## EVIDENCE OF EFFICIENT MARKETS

The notion of efficient markets is simply a theory that predicts how markets should work. Researchers at universities and advisors to brokerage houses spend a great deal of time studying this theory. Some find evidence supporting the theory that is overwhelming and accept it as given. For instance, there is a large body of evidence that considers the impact of various surprises on the market. One strand of this analysis examines the impact of monetary policy actions on stock prices. The efficient market view is that only unexpected changes in monetary policy affect stock prices since expected policy actions already are priced into the market. For instance, the evidence indicates that when monetary policy is tightened (interest rates raised) *unexpectedly*, stock prices often decline. On the other hand, if the change in policy was expected by market participants, stock prices show little response. Such evidence is consistent with the idea of market efficiency.

Another piece of evidence supporting efficient markets comes from mutual funds. If the efficient markets theory is correct, it is very difficult for someone to consistently "beat the market" as a whole. To do so requires that they consistently know things that others do not. If information flows freely to all, no one investor should have a greater ability to consistently predict the correct movement in stock prices. A testable implication of this view is that mutual funds that employ active managers—those who decide on what stocks the fund should buy (or sell)—should not do better (have higher returns) than funds that merely mimic the market as a whole.

Numerous studies have investigated the proposition that mutual fund managers should not consistently do better than the stock market as a whole. Almost without exception such analyses find that active mutual fund managers do not consistently beat the market over time. This has led many financial advisors to suggest that the best way to invest is to simply buy into a stock index mutual fund where the manager simply buys the stocks for the index in proportion to their importance in the market index. Such investing, for example the buying of index funds (see Chapter Three), is recommended due to the fact that the managers are unlikely to consistently beat the market.

EVIDENCE AGAINST MARKET EFFICIENCY: BEHAVIORAL FINANCE

The vast majority of financial economists subscribe, in one form or another, to the efficient markets theory of the stock market. In recent years, however, there is a growing number of financial economists, especially in academia, who question its validity. Perhaps, the best-known proponent of this view is Robert Shiller, author of *Irrational Exuberance*.[1] The main argument by this group is that investors and market participants do not always behave as rationally as predicted by the efficient markets theory.

Those that do not believe in efficient markets have some evidence to support their view. Consider the so-called January effect. The January effect refers to the observation that U.S. stock prices, on average, rise in January more than any other month of the year. This means that stock returns also are highest in January relative to any other month of the year. Proponents of the efficient market view argue that stock prices should not behave any differently in January than any other month of the year. After all, even if there are tax effects that make January different from other months, everyone knows when January is going to occur, so it should not be a surprise year in and year out. Those who believe in behavioral finance, however, point to this phenomenon as evidence that markets are not efficient.

Another example of something apparently inconsistent with efficient markets is the performance of stock prices for small companies relative to large companies. The theory of efficient markets suggests that an investor should not expect, all else the same, to receive a different return from buying stock in a small company than a large one. If everyone thought small company stock prices would do better than large companies, investors will drive up the stock prices of small companies. Their actions, based on their expectations, would force the investment returns on small and large company's stock into equality. The record in the United States indicates just the opposite: The average stock return is higher for small company stocks compared with stocks of larger companies.

Someone who believes in behavioral finance might point to this evidence and say "See, I told you markets are not efficient." Proponents of market efficiency offer a rational explanation. The comparison is not really fair because small company stocks are not as liquid; that is, they do not trade as often, on average, as the stock of a large corporation. Consequently, small company stocks are usually more difficult to buy and sell. It also is true that small company stock prices are more volatile than those of larger companies, so there is more risk in owning such stocks. And investors must be compensated for this risk. So, the comparison may not be an accurate one.

There are other examples of observed stock price activity that are difficult to reconcile with the efficient markets view. A popular one is that the stock market generally has a higher return in years when one of the original NFC teams wins the Super Bowl. This should not happen according to the efficient markets view: This information is known at the conclusion of the Super Bowl, so it should already be reflected in stock prices at that time. Observations like this are difficult to reconcile with the efficient markets view and may be anomalies. After all, not every theory is correct 100 percent of the time. As you might imagine, the two camps remain divided on how to interpret such anomalies. Behavioral finance offers it as evidence against market efficiency while others offer rational explanations of the anomalies.

## FUNDAMENTAL VERSUS TECHNICAL ANALYSIS

It is important to distinguish between the type of analysis that stock analysts rely on when selecting stocks that they think will do particularly well (or poorly for that matter). One type of selection process is referred to as fundamental analysis. Fundamental analysis finds its origin in an area closely akin to the efficient markets theory. A fundamental analyst aims at trying to guess the company's forthcoming financial statements better than other participants in the market. In other words, these analysts are looking to derive a better (more accurate) set of expectations (forecasts) than anyone else in the market. They select stocks that they think will perform better than others expect based on their forecast of key financial information, such as earnings growth. Market efficiency says that such analysts should not expect to make it a habit of beating the market, even though they may experience short-term success.

The other type of stock analysis is called technical analysis. An advisor who uses such analysis is often referred to as a technician. A technician usually starts with past stock price behavior and trading volume (the number of shares being bought and sold on a given day). Technicians believe that they can predict a stock's future performance from its past behavior and its trading volume. Like those in the behavioral finance camp, technicians do not believe that investors are completely rational. They argue, for example, that investors have a tendency to sell stocks that are "winners" (having risen in price) too early (before they have peaked). Similarly, investors tend to hold stocks that are "losers" (having fallen in price) too long. Technicians believe that past price and volume patterns can identify winners and losers. Of course, since technicians are only using known available data in distinguishing winners and losers, market efficiency proponents argue that investment strategies based on this approach also should not, over time, generate higher investment returns relative to the market.

## SUMMARY

It is useful to put the stock market into a context of today's investment environment. Some stocks are listed on public exchanges while others, most notably the privately traded stocks, are not. These latter stocks are an important, though often overlooked, aspect of today's financial system. Private stocks represent an important source of funds for smaller businesses, especially start-up companies. Because these stocks are not bought and sold on exchanges, they are neither as liquid nor are they as widely recognized or discussed, as publicly traded stocks.

Stock exchanges, where public stocks are traded, play a vital role in the economic and financial well-being of a country. In the United States, there are three major exchanges, the NYSE, the NASDAQ, and the AMEX. On these exchanges there are thousands of companies listed. To make help understand the general movements of the individual stock prices, broad stock price indexes are used. These include the popular DJIA and the S&P 500. More specialized indexes also exist, including the NASDAQ composite and the various Russell indexes of small firms.

Understanding how stock prices are determined—the information used to make buy and sell decision—is important to a successful investor. An overview of stock market efficiency provides a framework to understand why stock prices change over time. Basically, this idea is based on the notion that investors gather information about the company and what may affect its business. This information is used to form some expectation of the company's future success, and, from that, a "correct" stock price. Only when there is new evidence presented does the rational investor alter their expectation and, therefore, the stock price.

There is evidence both in favor and against this idea about how the stock market determines share prices. Whether investors adhere to this theory or not, whether they use technical or fundamental analysis to make their decision to buy and sell, it is important to understand these various aspects of the stock market if one is to make sense of the stock market.

## NOTE

1. Robert J. Shiller, *Irrational Exuberance* (Princeton, NJ: Princeton University Press, 2000).

# Five

# Recent Innovations in Stocks
# and Stock Markets

Many investors in the United States do not directly own stocks. Rather, they indirectly own them through a financial intermediary, such as a mutual fund. This chapter introduces you to the various basic funds, both new and old, used in the United States. Mutual funds, hedge funds, exchange-traded funds, and American Depository Receipts (ADRs) are all examples of investment vehicles that allow investors to have an indirect ownership of common stocks, not only of firms in this country, but throughout the world. This chapter also provides a basic introduction to the key derivative instruments that are used in association with common stock. Today there are futures contracts on stock indexes that actively trade on exchanges in the United States and, more recently, even futures contracts on individual company's stocks have begun trading. Finally, options contracts as a means for investors to use and manage their financial risks are discussed.

## MUTUAL FUNDS

Many investors do not buy individual stock directly but invest in stocks through a mutual fund. A mutual fund is a financial intermediary that accepts money from many investors and uses it to buy a variety of securities. The investor gets the advantage of the fund's ability to pick and choose large numbers of stocks, hopefully for a positive return. If the mutual fund primarily invests in stocks, then it is called a stock or equity fund. If it primarily invests in bonds, the fund is referred to as a bond fund. If the fund invests in both stocks and bonds, it is referred to as a balanced fund. There are almost as many mutual funds in the United States as there are publicly traded stocks. Mutual funds buy bonds as well as stocks, and they invest in stock traded outside of the United States. So the number mutual funds, while large, really is not too surprising.

Mutual funds are regulated by the Securities Exchange Commission (SEC). Funds are required to provide investors with a prospectus, informing investors how their dollars are invested and outlining the risks and potential returns. All mutual funds must calculate their net asset value, which amounts to the total value of all fund assets minus any of its liabilities divided by the number of shares outstanding for the fund. In other words, net asset value is the current excess value of fund assets that a shareholder has a claim to. If the value of the securities that the fund buys increases, then the fund's net asset value should increase and the shareholder realizes a positive return on their investment. Similarly, any dividends the fund receives from its stock holdings are added to the net asset value. Of course, for tax purposes, dividends, short-term capital gains, and long-term capital gains are treated differently by the shareholder. All mutual funds are required to calculate their net asset value on a daily basis.

### OPEN-ENDED FUNDS

Most mutual funds in the United States are open-ended mutual funds, meaning that there is no fixed number of shares offered by the fund. Open-ended mutual funds generally accept new investment monies and allow redemption on a daily basis. Shares of open-ended mutual funds are bought and sold at the net asset value of the fund. If the fund has no load, the fund is referred to as a no-load mutual fund. In somewhat rare cases, an open-end mutual fund stops accepting new investment money. In this case, the fund is confusingly called a closed, open-end fund. It is still an open-end fund since existing investors can redeem their investment monies from the fund on a daily basis. It is just closed to new, additional investors.

If a mutual fund has a load fee attached to it, the fund is called a load fund. Load fee refers to a front-end fee that is deducted by the fund from the money invested by the shareholder prior to the investment. A front-end load of 5 percent, for example, means that a mutual fund investor who sent $1,000 to the mutual fund would have $950 to invest in stocks and the $50 taken out would go to the mutual fund manager. An investor sending $1000 to a no-load mutual fund, in contrast, would see the entire $1,000 invested for their account by the fund. An investor putting money into a load fund might believe that they are getting a better mutual fund manager, since they already require a higher return relative to a no-load fund from the very outset. There is little evidence, however, indicating that load funds do better in terms of performance than no-load funds. Everything else equal, most investors wisely lean toward putting their money in no-load mutual funds.

While not all mutual funds have loads associated with them, all mutual funds do have expenses incurred in operating the fund. These costs are deducted prior to returning any investment gains to shareholders. All mutual fund investors should closely examine and consider the expenses of the mutual fund. These expenses include payments to the managers of the fund who select the securities bought by the fund, and expenses associated with maintaining the fund's offices, advertising, and promotions. Because expenses are deducted from the amount returned to shareholders, everything else equal, investors try to find a fund that minimizes the operating expenses of the fund. In their prospectus and other communication with investors, funds are required to inform investors of such expenses, generally stated as an expense ratio. The expense ratio measures the percent of total money invested by the fund made up of expenses. Index mutual funds (which you might remember from a previous chapter) invest in stocks that make up one of our stock indexes, and generally have the lowest expense ratio of all stock mutual funds. It is not uncommon for index mutual funds to have an expense ratio as low as 0.20 percent. Some other mutual funds pay their managers quite well and have significant advertising and operation expenses. It is not uncommon for such funds to have their expense ratio sometimes exceeding 3.00 percent. Generally, when a mutual fund reports its returns, it reports them prior to paying these expenses. In selecting a mutual fund, it is wise to consider the expense ratios: The lower the expense ratio, everything else equal, the greater the potential return from the investor's perspective.

## CLOSED-END FUNDS

There are not as many closed-end funds in the United States as open-end funds. Such funds serve a useful purpose for many investors, however. A closed-end fund, unlike an open-end fund, issues a fixed number of shares to investors at the outset of the fund's operations. The shares are sold to investors in a fashion similar to a corporation issuing stock at an initial public offering (IPO). With the money raised from the shares initially sold to investors, the fund managers buy securities, usually stocks or bonds.

An initial investor, however, cannot redeem their shares from the closed-end fund directly when they want to terminate their investment. The investor must go to a stock exchange and sell the shares, just like selling shares in a public corporation. A closed-end fund, like an open-end fund, is required to calculate the net asset value of the fund. But there is no guarantee that the investor will receive this value when selling their shares. Even though the market price of the fund usually does not stray too far from its net asset value, closed-end fund shares sell at prices different from their net asset value. When a closed-end fund sells in the market at a price above its net asset value, the fund's market price is at a premium. Alternatively, a closed-end fund sells at a discount when the market price is below the fund's net asset value.

Some closed-end funds invest in securities from outside of the United States. These funds are devoted to investing in developed as well as emerging markets. In addition, there are closed-end funds that invest in all varieties of bonds, including tax-exempt bonds, corporate bonds, and junk bonds.

## HEDGE FUNDS

Hedge funds have been around for many years but increased in popularity since the 1990s. The name is a bit of a misnomer. The term hedge often is used in finance to indicate a strategy of risk reduction; that is, attempting to lock in a predictable return on an investment. Hedge funds initially used investment strategies to reduce the risk of a portfolio. Today they are widely used for a much different investment objective.

To appreciate the role that hedge funds play in today's stock market it is useful to understand how a hedge fund may operate. For instance, a long-short strategy involves being long in certain stocks and short in others. Going long in a stock refers to buying the stock. Going short in a stock refers to borrowing a stock from another party and then selling the stock in the market. The borrower sells the stock initially at a price they expect to be a high price and plan to buy the stock back at a lower price in the future. When they buy the stock back at a lower price, they return the stock to the party they borrowed the stock from. Thus, investors take short positions in stocks that they anticipate will decline in price. If the investor is correct, they sell at a high price and buy at a low price. They are achieving their price gain, just in the reverse order of a long investor.

Another advantage of a short strategy is that if the general market falls in price (meaning the most stocks in the market decline), then a fund portfolio based on a long-short strategy will not decline in price as much as a completely long strategy. The fund using a long-short strategy will include some short positions that experience price declines. These price declines result in financial gains, so that long-short strategies are not as sensitive to market declines. Most initial hedge funds have some element of long-short strategy to them, thus giving the name hedge funds.

There are (in 2006) some 8,000 different hedge funds in the United States that manage approximately $1.5 trillion. As suggested above, it is best not to think of hedge funds as risk-reducing investment. Hedge funds do not face the same SEC oversight that mutual funds face. For example, unlike mutual funds, hedge funds do not have to provide investors with a prospectus defining the investments undertaken and the risks involved. In addition, to invest in a hedge fund, the investor must be a qualified investor, meaning that the individual investor meets certain financial thresholds. For example, the investor must either have annual income in excess of $250,000 or net worth of $1.5 million. Institutions such as pension funds and endowment are also large investors in hedge funds. It is best to think of hedge funds as lightly regulated funds that are available to certain investors.

Hedge funds employ numerous investment strategies other than the long-short strategy for which the term "hedge" was applied. In fact, many of these investment strategies do not reduce risk of loss, but actually are risk-increasing strategies. Broadly, hedge funds sometimes increase financial risk (potential for loss) by borrowing funds that are used (leveraged) to invest in derivatives. Mutual funds, for the most part, invest money that comes directly from shareholders. Hedge funds, in contrast, frequently engage in substantial borrowing and leverage. For example, when the now infamous hedge fund Long-Term Capital Management (LTCM) ran into financial difficulties in the fall of 1998, it came to light that the fund had borrowed about $96 of every $100 invested. In other words, shareholders in LTCM only put up about 4 percent of the money actually invested.

Such a strategy works well if the value of the assets owned by the fund is appreciating: The small group of hedge fund shareholders receives these gains. If the investments fall in value, however, as was the case for LTCM in the fall of 1998, the losses also are shared amongst a small group of investors and thus pose a greater risk for the fund becoming insolvent. The risk of loss is not borne only by investors in a hedge fund but also by those from whom the fund borrowed. In the case of LTCM, their faulty investment strategy would have cost banks and others sizeable losses if the firm had been allowed to fail. Employing leverage (borrowing some of the funds invested) provides a means that increases the potential reward and risk of a hedge fund's investment.

Another way that hedge funds increase the risk of loss is by employing derivative instruments. Later in this chapter, we will more fully describe some of the key derivative products tied to the stock market. Suffice it to say here that derivatives allow investors to put up relatively small amounts of money for the chance of a relatively large return on their investment. Of course the return can be positive or negative. Hedge funds that use derivatives increase the overall risk of their investment strategy. When they are right in their investment selections, this works to the advantage of their investors. But when they are wrong, this works against their investors and potentially others.

Since there are numerous hedge funds operating in the United States, we cannot say that the average hedge fund is riskier than a mutual fund. Some funds focus on capital preservation and use derivatives and other investment strategies to lower financial risks. Others do the opposite with the hope of obtaining greater returns for their shareholders, even though this also increases risk of financial loss. Because all hedge funds do not fall neatly into one or the other category, each one must be examined on an individual basis to properly access its risk profile.

## EXCHANGE-TRADED FUNDS

Exchange-traded funds (ETF) are relatively new financial instruments in financial markets. They are another type of index fund based on some major stock market index. For example, one of the most popular exchange-traded funds allows investors to invest in all the stocks that comprise the S&P 500 stock index. The fund, popularly known as the SPIDER, takes its name from the popular ETF Standard and Poor's Depository Receipts (SPDR). This fund takes investors' monies and invests a pro rata share of these funds in each of the 500 stocks in the S&P index. The fund really does not need to pay managers to determine asset selection since the intent is simply to buy, in the same proportion, those stocks comprising the S&P 500 index. The management expenses of such funds are generally quite small, adding to their popularity for general investment purposes.

ETFs are like closed-end funds in that they can be bought and sold on exchanges throughout the course of the day. Consequently, not every investor in an ETF on any given day buys in for the same price per share: Investors pay a different price than others as the price fluctuates up and down during the day. This is very different than open-end mutual fund investments where investors on any day pay the same price, the net asset value of the fund that day. Of course, competitive forces keep the market price of the ETF relatively close to the net asset value of the fund, since market participants can easily buy and sell the underlying stocks themselves.

Investment in ETFs allows investors to make one purchase, but their single share really amounts to an investment in a diversified portfolio of stocks. Not only is there an ETF devoted to the S&P 500 stock index, but there are funds devoted to, among others, the Dow-Jones Industrial Average (DJIA), the National Association of Securities Dealers Automated Quotation (NASDAQ), and the various Russell indexes. Some ETFs further partition their investment into specific sectors of an index. For example, one ETF allows investors to purchase part of the Russell 2000 index, those that are classified as value stocks, as opposed to growth stocks. Today, most ETFs are traded on the American Stock Exchange (AMEX), although a growing number are being introduced on the New York Stock Exchange (NYSE) and on the NASDAQ.

Because investors in ETFs are purchasing an individual share of the fund, there are certain tax advantages to this type of fund relative to investing in an open-end mutual fund. In particular, investors in ETFs have more discretion in realizing capital gains. This is because it is only when an investor sells their shares that they realize a gain or loss for tax purposes. An investor who holds their fund shares for a few years will not have to pay taxes on gains in appreciation until the stock is sold. This is not the case with an open-end mutual fund, where any gains or losses realized by the mutual fund are passed directly on to investors on an annual basis and taxed.

Due to the low cost of transacting in ETFs, the relatively low expenses associated with these investment strategies, and the tax advantages associated with them, the popularity of this type of fund has increased. Even some hedge fund managers are finding ETFs an attractive investment vehicle to add to their portfolio. ETFs expand the availability of investing in stocks in the United States and make investing in the equity market more attractive.

## AMERICAN DEPOSITORY RECEIPTS

American Depository Receipts (ADRs) are another relatively new addition to the financial markets. ADRs allow U.S. investors a simple means of investing in foreign stocks without going through the process of converting U.S. dollars into a foreign currency and then going to a foreign exchange to buy the stock. ADRs trade on U.S. stock exchanges and transactions are made in U.S. dollars. What makes ADRs attractive is that they do not invest in indexes of U.S. stocks but invest and own claims on foreign stocks. This allows investors to further diversify their investment portfolio. ADRs trade and settle according to U.S. exchange regulations, are quoted in the U.S. currency, and pay dividends in U.S. currency.

Let us use Teva Pharmaceutical Industries Ltd., an Israeli firm that specializes in the production, sale, and distribution of pharmaceutical products, to illustrate how an ADR works. A U.S. investor interested in investing in this firm does so through an ADR traded on the NASDAQ exchange under the ticker symbol TEVA (for TV junkies, this is not to be confused with TiVo!). The Bank of New York has created certificates based on its own investment in Teva. The Bank sells ownership claims to this via the TEVA ADR. A U.S. investor need only call a broker and place an order for this stock to receive pro rata claim on Teva, just as they would when purchasing a share of General Motors.

An enormous array of financial data is reported daily in newspapers and in "real-time" on-line. Photo courtesy of Corbis.

There are hundreds of ADRs traded in the United States. They represent a further globalization of financial markets, allowing U.S. investors to take an ownership claim in foreign enterprises without having to worry about foreign exchange matters and foreign brokerage firms.

## STOCK DERIVATIVES

Financial markets in the United States and other developed countries have witnessed the growing use of financial instruments that help manage the risks associated with investing in stocks. These new instruments allow investors to buy or sell stocks, not for immediate delivery, but for future delivery. This

In the 1990s, with instant and ubiquitous electronic access, on-line trading became popular. Photo courtesy of Corbis.

allows investors a mechanism to take some of the uncertainty out of stock investing. Other specialized investments also have been created that allow one to buy things that protect them against declines in the prices of stocks, sort of an insurance policy against financial loss. Although directly related to stock price movements, these new instruments are not traded on stock exchanges but on the commodities and futures exchanges. This section briefly describes the basics of those instruments, known as derivatives. They get this name because they derive their value from the behavior of underlying financial instruments, like stocks.

### FUTURES CONTRACTS

One of the oldest derivative instruments is the futures contract. These instruments started trading in the United States over 100 years ago and originally were used for the delivery of commodities and agriculture products, such as corn, wheat, sugar, silver, etc. Futures contracts require the buyer to take delivery of the underlying commodity at a future date. On the other side of the transaction, the contract calls on the seller to make delivery of the commodity on this same date. Thus, a futures contract is simply an arrangement for buyers and sellers to precommit to an exchange of the commodity (say, corn) for a specified price at a future date, rather than immediately.

As our financial system advanced, investors began to discover the usefulness of futures contracts tied to the stock market. For example, suppose that you know that you will receive a large cash settlement in six months' time and you know that you will invest this money in Google stock. This might appear to be a frustrating situation, especially if you think that Google stock might appreciate sharply before you are able to make your purchase. With a futures contract you can precommit to make the exchange at a future date; that is, today you can "lock in" the price for Google that you will have to pay six months from now. Regardless of what happens to Google's stock price between today and your actual purchase date, the price you pay per share has been preset. Such a futures contract reduces your financial risk.

What makes a futures contract particularly attractive is that exchanges like the Chicago Board of Trade and the Chicago Mercantile Exchange have developed very standardized futures contracts that call for delivery of very specific items, in specific amounts, and for delivery on very specific days of the year. Because these futures contracts are so standardized, buyers and sellers of these contracts really do not have to study the particulars of the contract and are comfortable in the knowledge of exactly what investment position they are taking. Moreover, these exchanges interpose themselves as the buyer to sellers of contracts and as the seller to buyers of contracts. Thus, while the exchanges seek to have a buyer for every seller of a futures contract, the identity of the counterparty is never relevant since the exchange literally stands as each party's opposite position. This is important because there has never been any failure of the major futures exchanges in the United States. Market participants are more willing to buy and sell, knowing that the exchange will make good on their contract.

The exchanges protect themselves from financial loss by requiring that each trader of a futures contract post a margin. The margin can come in the form of cash or securities and represents something that the exchange can claim should an investor not fulfill their obligation of the futures contract. Thus, to assure that one will take delivery at the stated price as a buyer of a futures contract, even if the market price of the underlying instrument has fallen, the exchange can claim those assets through the margin.

## Stock Index Futures Contracts

The first futures contracts directly tied to stocks that achieved much trading notoriety were stock index futures contracts. Recall the earlier discussion of different indexes in the United States: the DJIA, the S&P 500, the NASDAQ, and the Russell indexes. In the 1980s futures contracts based on each of these indexes were created. These contracts allow investors to either hedge overall market positions or speculate on the future path of the stock market as measured by these particular stock indexes. Initially, these stock index futures contracts were created primarily for large institutional investors. For example, the contract generally called for delivery of over $100,000 of the stocks in the index. The total amount that is deliverable is referred to as the notional value. This notional value was too large for most individual investors to consider stock index futures contracts as a viable investment vehicle. The notional value of the DJIA stock index futures contract today is ten times the value of the index, so if the index is at about 11,000, then the instrument calls for delivery of about $110,000 in stocks.

Not only is the notional value larger of most stock index futures contracts, but the corresponding dollar amount of margin needed to take a position in one of these contracts is also prohibitive for small investors. To take a long position in the stock index futures contract (take delivery at the future date) or to take a short position of the contract (make delivery at the future date), an investor would have to post a margin in the tens of thousands of dollars. Because the margin could easily be lost in one business day, such financial risk means that few individual investors use these contracts. Large institutions like hedge funds, pension plans, and endowments are the primary users out of these derivatives.

The major exchange in the United States that trades stock index futures contracts recently took action to widen the appeal of these contracts for small investors by creating mini stock index futures contracts. These contracts generally have about one-fifth the notional value and margin compared with traditional stock index futures contracts. The two most popular mini stock index futures contracts are the mini S&P 500, which calls for delivery of $50 times the value of the S&P 500 index, and the mini NASDAQ, which calls for delivery of $100 times the NASDAQ index. Smaller investors looking to hedge their stock exposure or to speculate on the future course of the stock market increasingly find these mini stock index futures contracts to be useful investments.

Stock index futures contracts and mini contracts have become popular enough and are traded in sufficient quantities that the major financial publications, like the *Wall Street Journal*, the *Financial Times*, and *Barron's*, provide information on trading in these instruments.

### Single Stock Futures Contracts

A very recent addition to the family of stock derivatives in the United States is the single-stock futures contract. As the name suggests, this futures contract calls for delivery of an individual stock instead of a basket of stocks that comprise some index. For example, an investor who wants to buy Dell stock in six months' time could do so by buying (going long) a single Dell stock futures contract. Recently, a new futures exchange called OneChicago began trading single stock futures contracts. These contracts call for delivery of 100 shares of the particular underlying stock, with delivery dates generally set for a few months in the future. The margin for these contracts is 20 percent of the notional value of the futures contract, where the notional value is essentially 100 times the individual stock price. OneChicago lists numerous individual stocks for which a futures position can be established, but the contract is really too new to say whether or not it is going to be used much by the investment community. Nonetheless, the single stock futures contract is likely to be a significant financial innovation in today's financial market.

### Options Contracts

Another important financial derivative for the stock market comes in the broad class of derivatives known as option contracts. Unlike a futures contract, which obligates both sides of the contract to either take or make delivery of the underlying asset at a future date, an options contract obligates only one party to act, giving the other party the option to do something. A long position in an option contract (the party buying an option contract) is the party given the option to act. They get the option that they will never exercise unless it is to their advantage for a price. The price of the option is referred to as the premium. The buyer of an option obligates the counter party (the seller) to do something. The seller of the option contract is referred to as either the writer of the option or the short position in the option.

The term premium is used to describe the price of an option. It also is the term used in the insurance industry to describe what a buyer of an insurance policy must pay. The same term is used in both contexts, because the buyer of an option contract can also be viewed as someone buying a certain type of insurance to protect them against financial loss. Buyers of option contracts are buying financial insurance; the seller of the option contract is the party providing it.

There are two different types of option contracts in the financial world. First, there are option contracts referred to as call options. Call options allow the buyer the option of the right to buy something at a preagreed upon price. Second, there are option contracts referred to as put options. A put option grants the buyer the option of the right to sell something at a preagreed upon price.

Let us first consider the call option in more detail. The seller of the call option is the party obligated to sell at the preagreed upon selling price, known as the exercise price. Consider a call option contract that allows the buyer to purchase 100 shares of Boeing stock at $95 a share. Assume that Boeing stock is currently trading at $90 per share. The buyer of the option contract can buy Boeing stock at $95 a share from the writer of the option anytime prior to the date the contract is said to expire, referred to as the expiration date. Of course, at today's stock price ($90), the buyer of the option would be foolish to exercise the option, since they could buy the stock cheaper in the market. In this case the buyer would not pay much per share for this option contract, surely less than $5 per share. This might change if the expiration date is far in the future, but most option contracts have expiration dates only a couple of months out.

Why would someone be willing to pay for a call option of this type where the exercise price is above the current market price? Referred to as an out-of-the-money option contract, it just does not make sense for the owner to exercise the option today. The answer is that an investor could view this option as an insurance policy against the stock's price increasing sharply in the future. Suppose an investor knows that $10,000 was coming their way in three months and that they will invest it in Boeing stock when received. The investor faces the risk that the price of Boeing stock increasing sharply between now and the time the money arrives. To insure against this occurrence damaging the investment return, the investor could buy a call option that allows them to buy Boeing stock at $95 per share. If something happened to drive the price of Boeing stock up sharply, say to $103, the buyer of the option would be happy that they had bought the call option. So, even an out-of-the-money call option has value to investors by offering insurance against certain possible events, in this case an increase in the rising stock price.

In addition to out-of-the-money option just described, there are in-the-money options. In-the-money call options have an exercise price that is below the stock's current market price. For example, if once again today's Boeing stock price is $90 and the call option had an exercise price of $88, this would be an in-the-money call option. In this case, ignoring the premium of the option, it would pay the long position to go ahead and exercise the option today. But as long as the option has an expiration date beyond today, the option will have a premium above the $2 difference in price. Thus, the holder of the option would probably wait until the expiration date to exercise the option contract. Finally, there are at-the-money option contracts. An at-the-money call option has an exercise price that is identical to the market price for the stock.

Buyers of call options on common stock take a certain position because it offers them insurance against price increases that they could not take advantage of themselves. Why would someone write a call option, or be the party obligated to sell the stock? The answer is similar to what we see in the insurance industry: firms are willing to provide insurance for the premium they receive. This is the same situation with call options. The writer, or the short position in a call option, gets the premium regardless of what happens in the future. The best case for the writer of a call option is that the option is never exercised. In this case, the writer of the option is never obligated to do anything at all since the option is never exercised: They just keep the premium when the option is unexercised. This is similar to the premium kept by your automobile insurance company when you do not have any accidents that require them to pay for repairs. Of course, the writer of the call option does bear the risk; in this case that the stock price will rise sharply in the market and they will have to provide the stock at a price below what it is currently selling for. The writer of a call option generally believes, however, that they are being compensated for bearing the risk that the underlying stock price might rise sharply.

Consider the other type of option contract, the put option. In the case of a put option the buyer of the option contract has the option to sell the underlying asset back to the writer of the option at a preagreed upon price (the exercise price). The seller or writer of the put option accepts the obligation for the premium that is given to them for the option contract. Buyers of option contracts are buying insurance, but in this case they are trying to protect themselves against falling prices of underlying common stock. Suppose you own 100 shares of General Electric (GE), currently trading at $34.10 per share. This investment is earmarked to pay for one of your children's college tuition next semester. So you don't want to lose all your investment, but you know that this is possible. Remember what happened to Enron stockholders? At the same time you don't want to sell the stock because you don't want to forgo the opportunity of financial gain if the stock price rises in the future.

In this situation you really need some downside protection. You want to be free to take advantage of the upside, but you do not want to live with the consequences of the stock price falling. With a put option contract, you have the ability to buy such protection. For example, suppose there were a put option available with an exercise price of $30.00 per share and an expiration date three months off. To buy this option you would have to pay the writer of the option a premium, but with the option you would have limited your maximum loss, ignoring the premium, to $410 [($34.10 − $30.00) × 100]. Thus, if the share price of GE fell to $27.74 immediately, you could exercise your option and force the writer to buy your stock at the exercise price of $30. For many investors, especially those with much of their wealth tied up in one or a few stocks and thus lacking the benefit of diversification, the cost of a put option is well worth the expense. They allow investors to "sleep a little more comfortably" knowing that they have some downside protection.

Put options contracts allow investors to better manage their risks. Those who own stocks and do not want to bear all the risk this ownership entails can reduce this risk by buying put option contracts. On the other hand, parties who want to take on more risk (and potentially greater returns) can easily do so by writing or selling put options. It should be noted that in addition to option contracts on individual common stocks as just described, the Chicago Board of Options Exchange (CBOE) also trades options on stock indexes.

## SUMMARY

Recent financial innovations in the United States have greatly enhanced the ways in which investors can invest in common stock. Mutual funds today are the "bread and butter" of investing for many. Rather than directly owning stocks, investors often own many different common stocks indirectly through mutual funds. There also are many new intermediaries that provide investment vehicles for investors. Hedge funds and exchange-traded funds are two of the more recent examples appearing on the financial landscape. Each allows investors to have an indirect stake in common stock. In addition, ADRs make it possible for U.S. investors to take a financial stake in foreign owned businesses without converting dollars into a foreign currency or worrying about transacting in foreign stock exchanges.

Other financial innovations that allow investors the opportunity to better manage their financial risks have come in the form of derivative instruments, such as futures and options contracts. For investors who seek to reduce their financial risks, these derivatives can be quite valuable. Of course, for the individuals seeking to reduce their financial risks with these derivatives, there must be someone out there willing to bear this risk.

# Six

# Regulation of the Stock Market

A complete review of the existing regulatory framework and the changes that have occurred throughout the history of the U.S. stock market would take us far beyond the scope of this book. Still, there are key regulations and regulatory bodies that merit attention. Before looking at specific regulations, it is useful to understand why securities markets are regulated at all.

## EXPLAINING REGULATION

It is common for stock exchanges to self-regulate. The New York Stock Exchange (NYSE), for instance, has a set of rules and regulations that its members must abide by. The same is true for the London Stock Exchange and the Hong Kong Stock Exchange. In each instance, an exchange-specific oversight body can levy penalties on brokers and dealers who do not follow the rules of the exchange.

The NYSE registers with the Securities and Exchange Commission (SEC) and is, therefore, subject to SEC oversight. (The role of the SEC is explained in greater detail later in this chapter.) Because of its registration with the SEC, the NYSE must agree to maintain a set of rules by which it regulates member activities. These rules have evolved over the past 200 years of trading activity. They often deal with how investors are treated and how the exchange will discipline brokers and dealers who violate the rules. For example, in the NYSE rules it states that "The Exchange may examine into the business conduct and financial condition of members, allied members, member organizations, employees of member organizations, approved persons and other broker-dealers that choose to be regulated by the Exchange." At another point the rules state that "The Exchange shall have jurisdiction over any and all other functions of its members . . . in order for the Exchange to comply with its statutory obligation as a Self Regulated Organization." The basic idea is that if a firm wishes to be an active member of the NYSE, it must abide by the rules. Failure to do so could lead the exchange to sanction the firm, an imposition of monetary penalties or even legal actions by the SEC.

Beyond self-imposed rules, why do governments establish broader constraints on the activity of securities markets? A look at government regulations suggests that the primary goal is to maintain some fairness in how the game is played. Among others, Allen and Herring note that this is much different than the approach taken to regulating other participants in the financial markets, such as banks. Bank regulation usually involves prohibiting the activity of individual banks.[1] It is not so much that governmental regulators fear the collapse of a single bank as much as they fear that a bank's collapse may lead other banks to fail as well. In the language of bank regulation, they want to reduce systemic risk.

Because a bank's assets and liabilities are matched in a unique way—banks only hold a small fraction of their liabilities (individual's checking accounts, for instance)—a spreading fear that banks are becoming less likely to remit deposits means that rational depositors will begin to withdraw funds before it is too late. This is the classic notion of a bank run. If everyone takes this attitude, customers' demand for funds swamps the bank's ability to satisfy the requests. Multiply this across many banks and you have systemic risk, or a contagion. When the central bank steps in to meet the demands of the depositors by infusing additional funds into the banking system, it is attempting to restore confidence in the banking system and allay any fears of potential loss. Deposit insurance represents another method by which the government attempts to calm the fears of depositors that their bank may close and their deposits disappear.

Regulating securities markets is different. For stock markets, it is not so much that the government wishes to prevent a single firm (say, stock broker) from bankruptcy as it is trying to influence the efficiency of the market. One of the key aspects of regulating the securities industry is to reduce asymmetric information between investors and dealers/brokers. For example, when someone buys the stock of a company, what power do they have to compel the company to supply detailed financial and business information? While large investors may have such power, most investors do not. This means that firms have an informational advantage that they may abuse. The most obvious misuse of this information is misreporting earnings to push stock prices higher. Stating earnings to be higher than expected (or than they actually are) raises a firm's stock price and, for those who hold it, gives them the unfair gain if they sell at the higher price. After those with inside information sell, the true earnings can be released and the stock price reacts accordingly (falls). Indeed, even though there is regulation against such practices, it still occurs: The most recent and notorious example is the Enron debacle.

Regulating the stock market has evolved partly into regulating the flow of information pertinent to making a well-informed investment decision. Unscrupulous traders cannot take advantage of unsophisticated investors. Investment information provided must follow certain standardized guidelines and the use of information not available to the general public—insider information—is not permitted. This latter aspect means that those with better information cannot take advantage of or profit from those without it. Interestingly, it was not until the 1990s that regulations against insider trading were imposed by foreign stock exchanges. The adoption of the Insider Trading Directive by the European Union in 1989 reflects an attempt to discourage such behavior on a broad scale. The Directive called on all member governments of the Union to outlaw insider trading activities in their securities markets. What is surprising is the amount of opposition from member governments there was to the Directive's passage. Even though such laws have existed in the United States for over a half-century, it was not until the Directive was passed that governments such as Germany and Italy contemplated imposing such trading restrictions.

Finally, an objective of regulating securities markets is to increase its informational efficiency. Allen and Herring suggest that since stock markets reflect decisions made by individuals using information, any regulation that increases the reliability of that information or reduces the cost in acquiring such reliable information will improve the efficiency of the market to set prices that accurately signal the underlying value of the firm.[2] Actions that reduce such efficiency—insider trading is one example—mean that stock prices do not properly reflect changes in the underlying values (the so-called fundamentals) of the firm. The bottom line is that if information in the market is not trustworthy because it is being manipulated by certain groups only to enrich themselves at others' expense, then investors may decide that the risk of investing is too great and withdraw their funds. If the overall level of investment activity is adversely affected, a key role of the stock market is thwarted and financial capital is not allocated as efficiently as possible.

With this background, how have regulations of the stock market developed in the United States? Significant regulatory changes seem to occur following significant events: A financial crisis is often times the trigger that brings change in regulation. This idea is a simple and informative approach that ties in with the previous discussion (Chapter Two) of how the stock market developed. Even though an outcome from the Panic of 1907 was the formation of the Federal Reserve System—not an insignificant result—it did not lead to substantial changes in how the stock market and its brokers and dealers operate. Consequently, the focus is on regulatory change stemming from the crashes of 1929, 1987, and 2000.

## REGULATORY CHANGES IN THE WAKE OF 1929

There were legislative attempts to reign in what some perceived as uncontrolled capitalism during the early part of the 20th century. A short list includes the "blue sky laws" passed by the Kansas legislature in 1911, the Transportation Act of 1920, and the Federal Water Power Act of 1920. Each affected stock trading, but not to the same magnitude as the laws passed in the 1930s. Indeed, it was the Crash of 1929 and the Great Depression that brought many to believe that unregulated capitalism was unstable. That is, left to its own devices, the dynamics of capitalism will generate booms and busts, both in economic activity and in the financial markets.

Since the markets and exchanges were largely self-regulated, any move to impose a blanket of federal government oversight of the securities markets "marked the end of the era of free enterprise capitalism and the beginning of the period of controlled capitalism."[3] This change stemmed from several major pieces of legislation passed following the election of Franklin Delano Roosevelt to the White House.

Following the 1929 crash it became increasingly clear that the stock market was subject to manipulation by large traders and company owners. Attempts to corner the market or manipulate stock were not unknown before the crash, and many believed that the events of 1929 simply repeated history. Beginning in 1933, the Senate Committee on Banking and Currency opened its investigation into the activities of the U.S. financial industry. The main objective of the investigation, which lasted seventeen months, was to root out causes of fraud and abuse, and to establish rules to improve the operation of both the securities markets and the banking system.

The Senate investigation became known as the Pecora investigation after the committee's chief examiner, Ferdinand Pecora. The committee summoned the biggest names on Wall Street and in banking to appear and to explain what had happened. After months of presentations, testimony, and reports, the committee made numerous recommendations. These recommendations were quickly converted into new laws that greatly affected the workings of the finance industry. Indeed, these laws provide the framework of rules and procedures that still determine how the stock market works.

## The Banking Act of 1933

A key piece of legislation derived from the Pecora investigations is the Banking Act of 1933, commonly referred to as Glass-Steagall after its co-sponsors. The Act separated commercial and investment banking by requiring commercial banks to divest themselves of their investment affiliates. The underlying rationale was that commercial banks in the 1920s used depositors' money to invest in the stock market. The widely held notion was that many banks were connected to the stock market through such investments. When the market crashed, it was argued, the commercial banking system was adversely affected—banks failed because of their investment losses—and this exacerbated the rate of bank failures and, in turn, the economic downturn. Separating banking from the stock market would remove that source of risk. Glass-Steagall was an attempt to insulate banking from the vagaries of the stock market. This act also created the Federal Deposit Insurance Corporation (FDIC) and instituted Regulation Q, which prohibited banks from paying explicit interest on checking accounts. (This latter regulation was overturned in 1980.)

Whether commercial bank activity in the stock market actually increased their risk of failure is open to debate. Current research indicates that trading in securities did not make banks more susceptible to failure. The fact is that only a small fraction of banks had large security operations and failed in the 1930 to 1933 period. In contrast, more than twenty-five percent of all national banks failed. Arguably, having an investment affiliate was not a good predictor of whether a bank would fail or remain open. But public opinion and political inertia required new laws to protect depositors. Good or bad, this act created the framework of the banking industry for the next half-century.

Not only did the Banking Act of 1933 force banks to divest often-times profitable components, but an unintended consequence was that it probably led to increased concentration in investment banking. Because of Glass-Steagall, the investment banking giants of First Boston Corporation, Morgan Stanley & Company, Drexel & Company, and Smith Barney & Company, to name a few, arose. These firms, along with the old-line investment houses of Kuhn, Loeb, and Lehman, controlled the lion's share of the investment banking business. Indeed, between 1934 and 1937, 57 percent of the new securities registered through the fledgling SEC were handled by the top six underwriter firms. The concentration in the bond market was equally great.[4] While the Banking Act of 1933 aimed at protecting commercial bank customers from risk, it also prevented banks from diversifying and increased the market power of investment banks.

### THE SECURITIES ACT OF 1933

The first major piece of legislation aimed specifically at the stock market from the Pecora investigation was the Securities Act of 1933. Sometimes referred to as the "truth in securities act," the objective was to increase the information available to investors purchasing stock and to reduce the amount of deceit and outright fraud of some brokers and traders when selling securities. This law required firms wishing to sell stocks to provide information about their line of business, a description of the security being sold, information about the management of the company, and financial statements pertaining to the company's operations. This latter requirement was given more weight by the fact that this information was certified by an independent accounting firm. In the recent wake of several large corporate collapses and scandals, several large accounting firms were held accountable for their failure to meet their role as independent auditors. They too collapsed. This episode led to changes in corporate accounting standards. Giving the Federal Trade Commission (FTC) oversight of the new rules, the act required underwriters to disclose more information to investors and oversight agencies.

The Securities Act of 1933 increased the transparency of trading securities. The key provisions of the 1933 act still are carried out by the SEC, a governing body that was created by the Securities and Exchange Act of 1934.

### THE SECURITIES AND EXCHANGE ACT OF 1934

The other major legislative change coming from the Pecora investigation is the Securities and Exchange Act of 1934. What this act and the Securities Act of 1933 did was to establish oversight of the securities industry by the federal government. Whereas the 1933 law focused on the flow of information from sellers to investors, the 1934 act was much broader in scope. As described in Allen and Herring,[5] the key areas that the 1934 Act focused on are:

- Publicly traded firms are required to file accounting returns periodically. Directors, officers, and holders of ten percent or more of the shares are also required to provide information on a regular basis.
- Solicitation of proxies is controlled.
- Regulation of tender offers was added in 1968.
- Oversight of the stock exchanges and over the counter markets. Self-regulation is encouraged through self-regulatory organizations such as the NYSE, the National Association of Securities Dealers, registered clearing agencies, and the Municipal Securities Rulemaking Board.

- Prevention of market manipulation.
- Prevention of insider trading.
- Control of credit to purchase securities by the Federal Reserve System.
- Regulation of clearance and settlement processes.
- Regulation of markets in municipal securities.

Although there are some aspects of the 1934 law that deal with information provision, its real aim is to regulate the trading of stocks. The Securities Exchange Act focuses on the exchange of securities by limiting insider trading, limiting speculative trading and credit, and regulating the actions of brokers and dealers. It accomplished all of this by creating the Securities and Exchange Commission (SEC).

## KEY LEGISLATION FOLLOWING 1934

There have been a number of laws passed since the 1930s that impact the operation and government oversight of the securities market in the United States. In 1940 two pieces of legislation were passed to further protect investors. The Investment Company Act of 1940 regulates companies engaged in trading or investing securities. This act increases the disclosure rules covering such firms, requiring them to inform the public of their financial condition and investment policies. For the most part, this law recognized potential conflicts of interest between firms that act as financial intermediaries and at the same time have publicly traded stock. The law sought to minimize such conflicts of interest.

In the same vein, when Congress passed the Investment Advisors Act of 1940, they were making sure that those engaged in the securities industry were abiding by the rules created in the Securities and Exchange Act of 1934. The Investment Advisors Act of 1940 required financial advisors to register with the SEC and, in doing so, conform to the rules established by that agency. With the proliferation of financial advisors in recent times, the act recently was amended to apply only to those advisors who had at least $25 million or more in financial assets under management.

Keeping with the notion that serious financial episodes often instigate regulatory change, passage of the Securities Investors Protection Act of 1970 was predictable. During 1969 and 1970 a number of brokerage firms faced financial distress. Some firms simply went bankrupt with their assets and accounts being absorbed by more solvent trading houses. Membership in the NYSE brought with it a financial safety net. That is, troubled brokerage houses could seek financial help from other members of the exchange.

But, as with any insurance program, severe drains on the fund led to problems.

Passed in December 1970, the Securities Investors Protection Act tried to buoy investor confidence in securities firms. One component of the act was to create the Securities Investor Protection Corporation (SIPC). Sponsored by the federal government but operated as a private corporation, the SIPC serves as the insurance company to securities investors. Using fees collected from member firms of national securities exchanges, the SIPC's purpose is to protect investors against losses stemming from actions taken by their brokerage house. That is, if a brokerage fails, investors' funds are protected up to a certain maximum. For instance, in 1970, the SIPC covered customer account losses up to $50,000: $30,000 for securities and a maximum of $20,000 for cash deposits held by the broker. This maximum coverage was increased over time. Today the maximum coverage is $500,000 with up to $100,000 for cash losses. To be clear, the SIPC covers losses of customers when their broker fails, not when they make a bad decision and buy a stock whose value declines.

## CIRCUIT BREAKERS IN THE POST–1987 MARKET

The stock market decline of 1987 seemed to leave few lasting economic scars. Even though there was loss of paper wealth by stockholders when the market plunged, unlike the Crash of 1929, a severe economic recession did not follow. This is partly because the stock market rallied quickly, regaining lost ground within a short period of time. The other reason is that the Federal Reserve acted swiftly in 1987 to forestall the downside economic effects of the stock market's decline. What came from the crash, however, was a change in regulations that affected not only the operations of equity markets, but also the futures and commodities markets.

The Crash of 1987 occurred in late October. By November 5, 1987, President Ronald Reagan signed Executive Order 12614 creating the Presidential Task Force on Market Mechanisms. The charge to the five-member task force, headed by Treasury Secretary Nicholas F. Brady, was broad:

The Task Force shall review relevant analyses of the current and long-term financial condition of the Nation's securities markets; identify problems that may threaten the short-term liquidity or long-term solvency of such markets; analyze potential solutions to such problems that will both assure the continued smooth functioning of free, fair, and competitive securities markets and maintain investor confidence in such markets; and provide appropriate recommendations to the President, to the Secretary of the Treasury, and to the Chairman of the Board of Governors of the Federal Reserve System.[6]

The findings of the Task Force were published in the so-called Brady Report. The report was far reaching in its analysis of prevailing trading practices in the securities industry. A key area upon which the report focused was the trading mechanisms used to exchange stock, especially how stock trading was increasingly linked to trading in the futures and commodities markets. With the advent of futures contracts on equity indexes, the equity and futures markets, once separated, were now linked. Since prices in the futures exchange (mainly the Chicago Mercantile Exchange) sometimes fluctuate widely, this can spill over to the NYSE market. One of the Brady Report's most important and controversial recommendation was the imposition of circuit breakers on trading activity when stock prices began to fall too rapidly and too far.

The basic idea of a circuit breaker is that if chaotic trading conditions like those of October 1987 arise, trading is halted until conditions are deemed appropriate for an orderly reopening of the market. In times of extreme price volatility, the market ceases to operate until conditions calm down. Supporters saw the trading halt as a time when investors, traders, specialists, and regulators could acquire additional information and assess the appropriateness of the prices being quoted in the market. It is argued that one reason for the break on October 19th and 20th of 1987 was the extreme volatility in stock prices.

If price changes do not reflect fundamental supply and demand conditions, they must be reflecting speculative behavior. For the average investor trying to make sense of the market's gyrations, prices no longer served the purpose of conveying reliable information. If investors are unsure of the informational content of prices, they may sell in a panic, dumping stocks simply to get out of the market and move to the sidelines. When massive sell orders occur as investors dump stocks, the physical mechanisms by which trades occur become overwhelmed. Those whose job it is to establish market prices and trends, the so-called specialists, are unable to keep up with the developments and establish orderly markets. This is what happened in 1987. The imposition of circuit breakers was viewed as a simple mechanism to prevent frenzied trading activity.

The Brady Report recommended that circuit breakers be thrown and trade halted for one hour when the Dow Jones Industrial Average (DJIA) index declined by 250 points, and for two hours if the index dropped by 400 points. (It is of interest to note that the report called for circuit breakers only during price *declines* even though there could be equal volatility on the upside.) The price declines necessary to invoke a trading halt were widened in 1997 to 350 and 550 points. This change was necessary because the original 250-point drop became a smaller and smaller percentage change as the level of the DJIA increased in the years following 1987. In other words, as the market continued to advance, a 250-point change became less unlikely and did not reflect a major meltdown in the trading mechanism. Though still a large change, a 250-point decline no longer disabled market makers and the flow of information. By 1998 it was recognized that creating point-based circuit breakers was inefficient and trading halts were tied to percentage changes in the index.

Regardless of the point change or the percentage change, circuit breakers have seldom been used. In fact, only after the price range was widened in 1997 did the DJIA move enough to trigger the circuit breaker. On October 27, 1997, the index dropped slightly more than 7 percent (554.26 points) and trading was halted temporarily. Interestingly, this decline would not have been large enough to halt trading under the changes to the circuit breakers adopted in February 1998. By then the minimum decline in the DJIA index before a trading halt was triggered was 10 percent. To put this into perspective, in early 2006, a trading halt would not occur unless the DJIA declined by over 1,000 points.

Response to the Brady Report was swift and generally unflattering. Some argued that imposition of circuit breakers reduced competition. Macey, for instance, argues that such externally imposed trading halts effectively "cartelize" the markets by not allowing them to compete against each other during times of price volatility.[7] That is, if the futures market is better able to deal with wide price swings, then it should get more business than competing markets that are less efficient at transmitting information. Throwing the circuit breaker in the stock market effectively obviates effective price competition between the markets. This lack of competition means that certain participants in the securities market, especially market specialists, gain at the expense of their customers during trading halts. Since specialists are able to set prices at the reopening of the market to their advantage, the regulation gives them an unfair advantage.

The difference between the regulatory changes spawned by the 1987 crash and the overhaul of the financial industry that followed the Crash of 1929 and the Great Depression is that the post-1987 changes have had little lasting effect. This is largely due to the fact that regulators, including the Federal Reserve, behaved very differently following the events of 1987 than they did earlier. Most importantly, the Federal Reserve moved quickly in the aftermath of the 1987 break to provide sufficient liquidity to the market: it acted as lender of last resort and shored up confidence that the market would continue to operate. Such was not the case in the post-1929 crash.

## REGULATORY CHANGE POST-2000 WORLD: A FOCUS ON CORPORATE FRAUD

Once the bull market ended in 2000, stocks drifted lower over the next couple of years. This downward drift was punctuated by declines in September 2001 and again in early 2002. Each was associated with world events

The corporate "perp": the symbol of business fraud in the 21st century, inspiring the Sarbanes-Oxley Act of 2002. Photo courtesy of Getty Images/Nick Koudis.

and not with developments in the stock market, per se. So what defined the earlier crashes—the rapid and steep decline in stock prices—is missing from the 2000 episode. Also missing from the 2000 break is the move to legislate the way the market operates. The widespread notion that the stock market needed "fixing" after the 2000 break just was not as prevalent as before. It may have been a speculative bubble that burst, but the basic functioning of the market was not questioned as it had been in previous episodes.

What did occur in the wake of the 2000 crash was a heightened awareness that the decline in stock prices was caused to some extent by corporate fraud. Stories began to appear concerning corporate fraud and accounting irregularities at companies like Enron and WorldCom. Although investor fraud and colorful characters have always been present in the securities industry, the extent of fraud and corporate malfeasance that was exposed topped historical comparisons. In the wake of these revelations, Congress moved swiftly to alter the rules by which business operated and to protect the investing public. On July 30, 2002, President George W. Bush signed into law the Sarbanes-Oxley Act of 2002. This act is hailed by some as one of the most important reforms in corporate practices since the 1930s. At its core, Sarbanes-Oxley attempts "to protect investors by improving the accuracy and reliability of corporate disclosures made pursuant to the securities laws, and for other purposes."

The aim of Sarbanes-Oxley is to reduce the asymmetric information problem that led to the collapse of large corporations. For example, the act focused on the failure of accounting firms to uphold proper auditing procedures. The act raised professional accounting standards by creating the Public Company Accounting Oversight Board. Sarbanes-Oxley raised the bar when it came to corporate audits by increasing the penalties for those convicted of corporate fraud. Of course, this also raised the cost of an audit, something about which corporations have complained since the act's passage.

With regard to the equities market, the act raised the level of informational disclosure required by publicly traded firms. For instance, firms with publicly traded stock now must disclose information about changes in their business or financial conditions more quickly than before. This accelerated disclosure gives the SEC more latitude in making decisions about the appropriateness of certain actions, such as trading in a company's stock by executive officers of the firm. Like previous legislation, the objective of Sarbanes-Oxley is to improve the information available to investors and regulators of securities markets.

## SECURITIES AND EXCHANGE COMMISSION

Throughout this discussion the SEC has been referred to but never really described. Stemming from the Securities Act of 1934, the SEC is the main regulator of the U.S. stock markets. In what follows, some detail on what the SEC covers and how it regulates the stock market is presented.

The SEC began operations in 1934 with President Franklin Roosevelt appointing Joseph P. Kennedy, matriarch of the Kennedy family, as its first chairman. This appointment was quite controversial on several grounds, not the least of which was the fact that Kennedy was widely known as an operator in the stock market, one who used the very same methods that the Securities Act of 1934 was attempting to curtail. After serving for two years, Kennedy was replaced by another Roosevelt loyalist James M. Landis who, after a relatively brief time, was replaced by William O. Douglas who left the SEC to become a Supreme Court justice and later its chief justice.

A creation of the 1934 act, the SEC is comprised of a governing body and several divisions. The governing body of the SEC consists of the commissioners. There are five commissioners, each appointed by the president and confirmed by the Senate. An SEC commissioner serves a maximum term of five years.. In an attempt to avoid blatant political packing of the commission, each commissioner's term is staggered; that is, June 5 of every year marks the end of a commissioner's term. Also, no more than three of the commissioners can be from one political party. The president appoints one of the commissioners to serve as the SEC's chairman.

**Key Securities Legislation**

1911   Kansas "blue sky laws"

1920   Transportation Act

1920   Federal Water Power Act

1933   The Banking Act of 1933 (Glass-Steagall) separated commercial and investment banking; created the Federal Deposit Insurance Corporation (FDIC)

1933   The Securities Act of 1933 increased information available to investors

1934   The Securities and Exchange Act of 1934 established oversight of the securities industry by the federal government through the Securities and Exchange Commission (SEC)

1940   The Investment Company Act of 1940 increased disclosure rules covering firms engaged in trading or investing securities

1940   Investment Advisors Act required financial advisors to register

1970   The Securities Investors Protection Act created the Securities Investor Protection Corporation (SIPC), insurance company to securities investors

1987   Presidential Task Force on Market Mechanisms produced the Brady Report, analyzing trading practices in the securities industry and imposing "circuit breakers" on trading activity

2002   The Sarbanes-Oxley Act enacted "to protect investors by improving the accuracy and reliability of corporate disclosures"

The SEC is made up of four divisions. Each division is responsible for some aspect of securities trading. The Corporate Division oversees the disclosure of corporate information regarding financial conditions of firms with publicly traded stock. One role of this division is to work with the Financial Accounting Standards Board (FASB) to establish and enforce uniform accounting standards across firms. Such uniform accounting practices help to improve investors' ability to understand the condition of a firm whose stock they may wish to purchase. This division also oversees the documents that publicly traded firms are required to file. For example, the division reviews documents filed by firms wishing to list stocks for the first time, it reviews annuals reports sent to shareholders and proxy materials distributed prior to annual meetings by firms, and it reviews and comments on requests by firms in the process of merging, or by firms attempting to takeover another firm. In all instances, the SEC's job is to make sure that proper information is disclosed that enables investors to make informed decisions.

The Corporate Division also is involved with translating federal legislation into working rules. While such legislation may provide a broad scope of what

Congress wishes to occur in financial markets, it is the SEC's job to see that these ideas are put into action. This "rulemaking" process has several steps. The first is known as the "concept release." As stated by the SEC, "a concept release is issued describing the area of interest and the Commission's concern and usually identifying different approaches to addressing the problem." In other words, at this stage of the rulemaking process, the SEC is trying to determine the scope of the problem and how it should be dealt with. At this stage the SEC invites public comment to help the SEC form a plan of action. Once this plan is established, the next step is taken. This is the "rule proposal" stage. At this point in the process, the SEC has established a detailed rule proposal based on information received from the concept release stage. The rule proposal stage is much more concrete than the concept stage: The rule is specific in its objective and the methods the SEC plans to use to achieve that objective. This stage also is made public, with a response period of thirty to sixty days. Using public input and based on internal discussion, a final rule is created, which is presented to the SEC commission for consideration. This final stage is the "rule adoption" stage. If adopted, the rule becomes part of the SEC's arsenal to promote sound and safe securities markets.

The SEC's Division of Market Regulation has the task of making sure that securities markets operate in an orderly and efficient manner. It is this division that regulates the various stock exchanges in the United States. Even though the different exchanges—the NYSE, the American Stock Exchange (AMEX), and the National Association of Securities Dealers Automated Quotation (NASDAQ)—are self-regulated, the SEC has oversight powers over the operations of the exchanges. This division also oversees operations of the SIPC. A private corporation, the SIPC is to the securities industry what the FDIC is to banking. The SIPC insures customers' securities and cash accounts that reside with member brokerages.

Oversight of investment managers comes under the umbrella of the Division of Investment Management. Their goal is to protect investors from adverse behavior by investment advisors, including mutual funds. This division also oversees the activity of utility holding companies, stemming from powers granted under the Public Utility Holding Company Act of 1935. In this role the SEC ensures uniformity in financial reporting, accounting rules, auditing, etc. of these holding companies.

Last, the Division of Enforcement is given the responsibility to investigate violations of securities law. The SEC has civil enforcement authority and brings action against violators in Federal District Court. Such actions are often injunctions to force companies to stop some practice that violates SEC rules. Sometimes, the SEC may pursue more rigorous action, even to the point of requiring firms to return to investors profits that were obtained through some breach of SEC rules, an action given the unlovely term "disgorgement." Violations that trigger an SEC action include insider trading, manipulating stock prices, stealing customer securities and/or funds, and the sale of securities without being properly registered.

To increase transparency, the SEC requires companies listing their stock to follow certain rules. This responsibility comes from the Securities Act of 1933. To achieve its goal of transparency in securities trading, firms with publicly traded stock must register with the SEC. The purpose is to create a common body of information that investors can use when making their decisions. When any company registers with the SEC, it is required to provide a given set of information, including financial statements by outside accountants, who the management of the company is, and what the company's business is. While these may seem obvious pieces of information that any investor requires before buying a stock, the SEC's registration requirement creates uniformity in the information being provided. It makes it easier for investors to compare one firm to another. It also creates a basis on which the SEC can later bring legal actions against firms that knowingly falsify their registration documents, or used improperly acquired financial statements from outside auditors. Such statements are accessible electronically using the Electronic Data Gathering, Analysis, and Retrieval system (EDGAR). Through EDGAR, firms can electronically submit the necessary forms and the public can access them. As with many other SEC activities, EDGAR improves the transparency of transactions and increases the comparability and speed with which information is available.

## SUMMARY

Current governmental regulation of the U.S. stock market evolved from several significant events. For the most part, the foundation of existing regulations stemmed from the government's reaction to the Crash of 1929. That debacle exposed a number of flaws in the securities market, especially in terms of stock price manipulation and the use of outright fraud. The regulations passed in 1933 and 1934, and the creation of the SEC altered the manner in which the stock market operated. Even though there have been numerous amendments to these original laws, they effectively delineate how the market operates. And, if mimicry is flattery, similar regulations and regulatory bodies have been created in most other major securities markets around the world.

## NOTES

1. Franklin Allen and Richard Herring, "Banking Regulation versus Securities Market Regulation" (The Wharton School Financial Institutions Center, Working paper, 2001), 1–29.

2. Ibid.

3. Robert Sobel, *The Big Board: A History of the New York Stock Market* (New York: Free Press, 1965), 299.

4. Ibid., 308.

5. Allen and Herring, "Banking Regulation versus Securities Market Regulation."

6. www.reagan.utexas.edu/archives/speeches/1987/110587k.htm.

7. Johnathan R. Macey, "Regulation and Disaster: Some Observations in the Context of Systemic Risk" (Brookings-Wharton Papers on Financial Services, 1998).

# Seven

## Stock Markets Abroad

Which is the world's largest stock exchange? The answer to that question depends on which measure is used. If it is market capitalization—the number of outstanding shares multiplied by their market value—then the New York Stock Exchange (NYSE) is by far the largest. If the measure is number of companies listed, the NYSE is no longer number one. In fact, the National Association of Securities Dealers Automated Quotation (NASDAQ) exchange has more companies listed than the NYSE. How many exchanges are there around the world? Let us just say that most countries today have a stock exchange and even though their daily operations often differ from those of the NYSE, their regulations are not identical and the sizes vary considerably, they all are geared to the efficient distribution of financial assets.

The history and workings of a select group of foreign stock exchanges is one topic for this chapter. Since there are literally hundreds of stock exchanges around the world, the coverage is limited to those often found referenced in the financial press. Some of the best known are the stock exchanges of Hong Kong, London, and Tokyo. Because of their size, long history, and regional importance, our brief survey includes the stock exchanges in Frankfurt and Toronto too. Missing from this list are exchanges that have long histories but have fallen from a level of importance that justifies their inclusion. Obvious candidates are the Amsterdam—the oldest stock market in the world—and the Paris exchanges. One reason for excluding them as separate entries is the fact that in 2000 these exchanges merged with the exchange in Brussels to form the cross-border exchange called Euronext. We will touch on the significance of the Euronext exchange.

In addition to providing some history of these exchanges, the role that stock markets (and financial markets in general) play in economic development is explored. Indeed, the evidence suggests that opening a stock market spurs economic growth, something that undoubtedly is of great concern to policymakers everywhere, especially those in newly emerging market economies.

## COMPARING STOCK MARKETS

To get a feel for the comparative size of stock exchanges around the world, Table 7.1 lists some of the major markets ranked by their market capitalization (in U.S. dollars) at the end of 2004. The data show that the NYSE is by far the largest exchange. The fact that the NYSE has a capitalization of about $12.7 trillion means that it is almost four times larger than the next largest exchange, which is the Tokyo exchange. Notice that the NASDAQ exchange ranks third in this list, ahead of the London, German, and Hong Kong exchanges. This illustrates the sheer size of the U.S. stock market relative to the rest of the world.

Another point to make is that some exchanges listed in Table 7.1 did not even exist until a few years ago. The fifth largest exchange—Euronext—came about in 2000 when exchanges in Amsterdam, Brussels, and Paris merged. Operating through subsidiary exchanges in these countries, Euronext N.V., a holding company incorporated in the Netherlands, is a true cross-border exchange. It is likely to be a portent of the future as exchanges in one country buy exchanges located in other countries.

**TABLE 7.1**
**Exchanges Ranked by Market Capitalization in U.S. Dollars, End of 2004**

| Exchange | Capitalization (millions of U.S. $) |
|---|---|
| NYSE | $12,707,578 |
| Tokyo | 3,557,674 |
| NASDAQ | 3,532,912 |
| London | 2,865,243 |
| Euronext | 2,441,261 |
| Osaka | 2,287,047 |
| Deutsche Borse (Frankfurt) | 1,194,516 |
| Toronto | 1,177,517 |
| Hong Kong | 861,462 |
| Swiss Exchange | 826,040 |

*Source:* World Federation of Exchanges (2004).

## A BRIEF HISTORY OF FOREIGN STOCK EXCHANGES

### TOKYO EXCHANGE

In terms of market capitalization and number of companies listed, the Tokyo exchange ranks as one of the largest in the world. As shown in Table 7.1, at the end of 2004, it ranked second only to the NYSE in terms of market capitalization. The Tokyo exchange is quite a success story, especially when one considers the fact that the market essentially began anew following World War II.

The history of the Tokyo exchange dates back to the 1800s.[1] In 1878 the Stock Exchange Ordinance was enacted, creating the Tokyo Stock Exchange Company, Ltd. The exchange's modern history, however, dates from the 1940s. In 1947 the Securities and Exchange Law, modeled after U.S. securities laws, was passed. Stock trading was slow immediately following the war, although by the late 1940s eight exchanges were operating throughout Japan. Over time a series of mergers occurred. Today there are five stock exchanges in Japan with the Tokyo exchange the largest. The second largest exchange in Japan is located in Osaka, a market that itself ranks sixth in the world in terms of market capitalization in 2004 (see Table 7.1). This means that Japan is the only other country to have two exchanges listed in the top ten largest.

Trading on the Tokyo exchange increased rapidly after the war. For example, trading volume that stood at 512 million shares in 1950 increased to over 102 billion shares by 1980. By 2004 the exchange topped 378 billion shares traded, accounting for about 97 percent of all trades in the Japanese stock exchanges.[2]

Like most markets in the dynamic world of finance, the Tokyo exchange experienced a number of changes. Historically, the major corporations traded in what is referred to as the "First Section." Stocks in the First Section traded at specific locations on the exchange's trading floor, with stocks from like industries. The expansion of the market led to the creation of the Second Section in 1961. Stocks in the Second Section tend to be those of smaller, newer companies. And in 1983 the exchange opened the Third Section, trading stocks in companies similar to those listed in the NASDAQ exchange in the United States.

It was believed by many in the 1980s that the Japanese economy eventually would dominate the global economy. Its rapid pace of economic growth fueled rapidly rising stock prices. The Tokyo Stock Price Index (TOPIX), introduced in 1969, rose from 148 in 1970 to 2,881 by 1989. In similar fashion, the better-known Nikkei 225 index increased a staggering 1,858 percent between 1970 and 1989. (By comparison, the Dow Jones

Industrial Average [DJIA] increased about 233 percent over the same time.)
But the rapid rise of the market, and the economy, did not last. The Japanese
economy suffered a decade-long recession in the 1990s and there were
widespread financial failures. Indeed, the Japanese economy is only now
(2006) beginning to recover after almost fifteen years of tepid economic
growth. This failure to sustain economic growth is reflected in stock values:
At the end of 2004, the TOPIX index was less than half its 1989 value and
the Nikkei 225 index was less than one-third its 1989 peak. Even though the
Tokyo Exchange has endured a prolonged period of hardship, it remains a
key market in Asia and the global financial system.

## LONDON EXCHANGE

London has been a world financial center for many years.[3] Tracing its
beginnings back to the late 1690s when lists of stocks were issued in Jonathan's Coffee-House, the history of the London Exchange is similar to the
NYSE. For example, the initial trading of stocks — the term stock in London
was used to describe fixed income securities, not equities — was unorganized,
like the trading that took place outside on Wall Street. Organized trading in
the London Exchange did not really begin until 1761 when about 150
brokers and jobbers formed a group to buy and sell shares, still at Jonathan's
Coffee-House. It was not until 1801 when the first regulated exchange opened
for business, and not until 1854 that the first stock exchange building was
erected.

Although the London Exchange experienced a series of advances and setbacks in its long history, one of the most important recent events occurred in
1986 with the so-called Big Bang. The Big Bang was a major change in the
regulation of the London Exchange. The Big Bang sought to reform the club-
like nature of the exchange. Among the many changes was allowing all firms to
become brokers/dealers. Historically, trades came through brokers who dealt
with jobbers (essentially market makers on the floor). The Big Bang permitted
the kind of dual function similar to activity of specialists on the floor of the
NYSE. The Big Bang also changed the nature of the firms making up the
exchange's membership: After 1986 member firms could be owned by foreign
corporations. Although the Big Bang deregulated some activities of the exchange, it also produced a new batch of regulations. This in part came from
the creation of the Securities and Investment Board (SIB). The SIB was given
broad supervisory and regulatory powers over the exchange and its members,
similar to the powers of the Securities and Exchange Commission (SEC) in
the United States.

The London Stock Exchange, one of dozens of stock exchanges around the world. Photo courtesy of Getty Images/PhotoLink.

The London Exchange remains as one of the largest in the world. With a market capitalization of over $2.8 trillion at the end of 2004, the exchange ranks fourth in size. In terms of listed companies, the exchange is the third largest in the world behind the NASDAQ and Toronto exchanges.

## Hong Kong Exchange

The Hong Kong stock exchange is one of the most important financial markets in Asia. Today's official stock exchange—the Hong Kong Exchanges & Clearing Ltd (HKEx)—represents the latest chapter in a long history of stock trading in Hong Kong. The stock exchange began much like those in other countries.[4] Originally an informal gathering of traders, probably beginning in the mid-1800s, a formal exchange was formed in 1891 by the Association of Stockbrokers. Through the years, other exchanges opened in Hong Kong to meet increased needs for financial capital. A second exchange opened in 1921 and operated until shortly after World War II. The two merged in 1947 to form the Hong Kong Stock Exchange. As the economic development of Asia started to boom in the 1960s, so too did trading activity on the Hong Kong exchange. In fact, the increased need for financing business and industry gave rise to the opening of several additional stock exchanges in Hong Kong.

The development of Hong Kong's financial sector took off in the 1960s and the 1970s. One explanation, other than the demand for financial assets and investment capital, was the largely market-driven regulation of the exchange. That is, compared to stock markets in other countries, governmental oversight of the stock market in Hong Kong was minimal. This changed dramatically in 1974, when the overall market suffered a huge loss in value. As often occurs following significant financial market calamities, there arose a call for increased regulation of the exchange and the financial industry in general. In 1974 the Securities Ordinance was enacted to provide greater governmental oversight of securities trading. One reform was to create the Office of the Commissioner of Securities. The job of the Office was to ensure conformity with the Securities Law and to regulate trading activity on the Hong Kong exchanges. Further regulation occurred in 1980 with the passage of the Stock Exchange Unification Ordinance. This ordinance was enacted to standardize industry actions and information. Partly a result of the increased regulation, in April of 1986, several exchanges merged to form the Stock Exchange of Hong Kong (SEHK).

The global crash in stock prices in 1987 ushered in more changes in the Hong Kong stock market. The counterpart to the Brady Commission in the United States (see Chapter Six) was Hong Kong's Securities Review Committee. Like the Brady Commission, the committee's 1988 report took a hard look at stock trading on the Hong Kong exchanges. It was full of recriminations about existing trading practices and called for increased regulation. In its report, the commission partly blamed the crash on the SEHK's management and lax regulation of trading. Although there were many specific points raised in the report, the committee focused its reforms on the self-regulatory style under which the SEHK had operated. The committee called for restructuring the management of the SEHK, for altering the listing procedures then used, that an oversight body of technically trained professionals be created, and that a separate watchdog group be formed to oversee exchange activity. By 1989 the Securities and Futures Commission (SFC) was created to replace the Office of the Commissioner of Securities and to oversee these expanded responsibilities.

Like other exchanges, not only has the SEHK come under increased regulatory scrutiny but it also faced increased global competition. To meet this competition, the SEHK and the Hong Kong Futures Exchange merged in 2000 with the Hong Kong Securities Clearing Co. The combination formed the holding company Hong Kong Exchanges & Clearing Ltd., better known by its acronym HEKx. The best-known market index of HEKx is the Hang

Seng Index. The Hang Seng Index, which began in 1969, consists of the thirty-three largest firms traded on the stock exchange. These firms are chosen to represent four industry groups, including commerce, finance, property, and utilities. The firms in the index comprise about seventy percent of the exchange's total market capitalization. With an initial value of 100 on July 31, 1964, the value of the Hang Seng Index was slightly over 15,500 by early 2006.

## Frankfurt Exchange

The stock exchange located in Frankfurt is the largest of eight exchanges operating in Germany. The Frankfurt Wertpapierborse (Frankfurt Stock Exchange) has existed, in one form or another, since the sixteenth century. The operating body of the exchange is the Deutsche Borse AG.

The Frankfurt exchange's history stems from the fact that Frankfurt has long been a center for trade and commerce.[5] The beginnings of the exchange coincided with an annual fall festival at which merchants from many different countries met to sell their goods. The beginning of the exchange in Frankfurt, unlike the others reviewed, was oriented to setting exchange rates for currencies used by traders. Although it is believed that the initial meeting of merchants to set these rates occurred in 1585, it was not until 1682 that the Exchange Rules and Regulations was drawn up and enacted. This date probably marks the truest beginning of the stock exchange.

In the early 1800s the Frankfurt exchange was comparable with those in London and Paris in terms of its financial importance. Even as the exchange grew, however, its progress was markedly different than the exchanges in London or the United States. As late as 1850 brokers at the Frankfurt exchange primarily traded government bonds. It was not until about 1880 when the New Stock Exchange opened that the conversion to trading corporate stocks occurred. Even with the increased activity in stock trading, the Frankfurt exchange remained primarily a market for domestic and international bonds. Facing increased competition from the stock exchange in Berlin, the Frankfurt exchange aggressively moved to stock trading by the late 1800s.

The first half of the 1900s was not good to the exchange. In World War I the exchange was hit especially hard as domestic investors sold off their foreign bonds and stocks and reduced their trading activity. The economic events following the war and the calamity of the Great Depression further reduced activity on the exchange. In 1933, when the Nazi regime rose to power, their centralized plan resulted in a further loss of status for the Frankfurt exchange. Not only had Frankfurt declined as an international financial center, but domestic government actions also hindered the use of stocks to fund investment projects in Germany.

Although the exchange continued to operate during World War II, it no longer was a financial powerhouse. The exchange opened in the fall of 1945 after a brief hiatus, becoming one of the first German exchanges to renew trading operations after the war. The importance of the exchange in the reconstruction of the German economy was recognized by Allied occupiers. As the economy recovered from the devastation of the war, so too did the exchange.

The Frankfurt exchange has remained competitive by introducing new products. In 1988 the exchange introduced the DAX, a blue-chip stock index that remains the main indicator of stock market activity in Germany. As markets expanded, so did the need for more specialized indexes. In 1997 the Neuer Market was established to focus on stocks of smaller companies. Within the past several years, the exchange launched the TecDAX, a stock index compiled largely of blue-chip technology firms.

Like other exchanges, the Frankfurt exchange also increased the transparency of its trading rules about that time. There are several layers of regulatory oversight in the Frankfurt exchange. At the federal level, the Market Supervisory Authority (MSA) operates much like the SEC in the United States. The MSA works to ensure fair and orderly trading, protecting investors from unscrupulous brokers and traders. The Federal Financial Supervisory Authority (BaFin) investigates charges of insider trading and instances where disclosure rules have been violated. It is the BaFin that prosecutes market manipulators. The Trading Surveillance Office (HUSt) oversees the process by which prices are set and how trading occurs on the floor through the electronic Xetra and Eurex trading systems. The HUSt has investigative powers that enable it to refer problems to the MSA for action. Finally, the Exchange Supervisory Body provides oversight at the state level.

TORONTO EXCHANGE

The beginning of the Toronto Stock Exchange is much like that of others: an informal gathering of brokers for the purpose of trading.[6] The assemblage and formation of an exchange is done to establish trading rules and to create a more efficient form of raising capital. And so it was with the Toronto exchange. In 1861 about two dozen brokers gathered and resolved to establish an organization in which trading would be carried out only by members of the group. There were only sixteen securities listed on the exchange at the time. But the number of securities and of members soon increased. Within a decade the number of brokers had increased and there were fourteen different firms. One indication of the increased value of a membership on the exchange is the rising price to join: An exchange membership that sold for $5 (Canadian) in 1861 jumped to $250 by 1871.

During the late 1800s the exchange increased in size and importance. In 1878 this was recognized by the Ontario legislature when they incorporated the exchange. By an act of the legislature, it officially became the Toronto Stock Exchange. At the turn of the new century the number of listed stocks stood at 100 companies and annual trading volume reached 1 million shares. The value of being a member again is demonstrated by the skyrocketing value of a seat on the exchange. The price of membership was $12,000 in 1901 compared to only $250 some thirty years earlier.

The early 1900s witnessed further development of the exchange. The volume of trading and the market's capitalization continued to grow and new trading technologies were introduced. In 1913, for example, the print-out ticker was introduced to record changes in stock prices as they traded. Like exchanges in the United States, the Toronto exchange suffered with the onset of the Great Depression. In relative terms, however, the financial damage in Toronto was not as severe as in the United States. For instance, by 1933, no Toronto stock exchange member had defaulted on its obligations to clients. This is in stark contrast to the problems faced by U.S. brokers (see Chapter Two). The fact that the Toronto exchange was not hit as hard by the Depression is indicated by the fact that by 1936, it had grown to be the third largest in North America.

The technological growth of the exchange mirrors that of others, though the Toronto exchange recorded some firsts. In the late 1970s the exchange implemented a new trading system called Computer Assisted Trading System (CATS). One of the first exchanges to use such computerized trading, this helped push trading volume even higher. In 1996 the exchange introduced decimal trading, long before the NYSE made the conversion. And in 1997 the Toronto market completed its move to floorless, electronic trading.

In 1977 the Toronto exchange launched a new stock index, the TSE 300 Composite Index. This marked the first of several indexes created to reflect the expanding nature of the capital and equity markets in Canada. Since the 1990s, several more indexes were introduced. Reflecting the development of equity trading and financial markets in Canada, several mergers of exchanges also has occurred. In 1999 the Vancouver and Alberta exchanges merged to form the Canadian Venture Exchange (CDNX). The focus of the CDNX was on trading in small-firm equities. CDNX later acquired the equity trading portions of the Montreal and Winnipeg exchanges. In two short years, however, the Toronto exchange—which converted to a for-profit organization in 2000—acquired CDNX.

Other mergers and acquisitions have transpired since 2000. In 2002, Standard and Poor's together with the TSX Group—the owners of the Toronto exchange—launched the S&P/TSX Venture Composite Index.

Annual trading volume soared to over 46 billion shares. The TSX Group in fact launched its own initial public offering (IPO) in September 2002, and by early 2003, the TSX Group declared its first dividend. In a move to increase the efficiency of trading, in March 2004, the TSX Group started Market on Close to help stabilize orders and pricing at the end of the trading day. With trading topping out at over 7 billion shares in January 2004, such improvements in efficiency and information transmission are improvements in reducing the informational asymmetries that sometimes occur in equity markets.

EURONEXT EXCHANGE

If this book was written ten years ago, there would be entries for other exchanges, like those in Amsterdam and Paris. The landscape of stock exchanges has changed quite dramatically over the past decade, however. A major change occurred in September 2000 when the stock exchanges of Paris, Amsterdam, and Brussels merged to form Euronext N.V., the first cross-border exchange in Europe.[7]

This cross-border exchange represents the likely trend of stock markets in the future: a holding company (like Euronext N. V.) that operates subsidiary exchanges in several different countries. This provides the exchange with an increased global reach, increases the liquidity of the market, and lowers transaction costs of trading across political boundaries. Since 2000, Euronext has grown through further consolidations to become one of the largest exchanges in the global financial community. In 2002, Euronext acquired the London International Financial Futures and Options Exchange (LIFFE) and merged with the Lisbon stock exchange, Bolsa de Valores de Lisbona e Porto (BVLP). Euronext represents the future of stock exchanges: increased consolidation across financial and political boundaries.

SUMMARY

The foregoing discussion provides some background on the various major stock exchanges around the world. It was mentioned that a trend occurring over the past few years is the consolidation of trading operations. The Euronext exchange is one such example. The bidding for the London Stock Exchange by the NASDAQ, the NYSE, the Deustsche Borse, and the Macquarie Bank of Australia in early 2006 indicates the changing nature of the exchanges: Once entities that traded regional or national stocks, exchanges have moved on to global proportions. More and more exchanges are moving away from private organizations with exclusive membership to publicly traded corporations. The most recent such change is the IPO by the NYSE in early 2006. Finally, another trend is away from the historic trading floor to electronic exchanges. The NASDAQ market has always been such an exchange and, with its merger with Archipelago in 2006, the NYSE is moving in that direction.

## ARE STOCK PRICES RELATED?

If the connection between national exchanges is becoming increasingly intertwined, is the same true of the stocks traded on them? That is, do stock prices in the various markets move together? At first blush the answer is yes, of course. After all, the morning stock market report heard on many radio stations or viewed during early newscasts often times relate movements in stock prices across markets. How often does one hear something like "U.S. stock prices are poised to open higher given the higher close in most Asian markets." Since the important Tokyo and Hong Kong markets close before the U.S. market opens, how their trading day fared sometimes is used as a bellwether for U.S. stocks. It should not be, however.

Stock prices can be thought of as an investor's valuation of expected future dividends or a firm's stream of future revenues. For stock prices to be linked internationally, the expected returns on stocks from the different markets must be identical when measured in a common currency. That is, an investor in the United States measures expected returns in terms of dollars. When comparing the returns of various stocks of U.S. or foreign companies, the investor will compare dollar denominated returns.

For the sake of argument, suppose that the expected return from holding a share of a domestic company is exactly equal to the expected return from holding a share of a foreign firm. Even under that condition, stock prices in different national markets will not be related over time. One reason is that individual firms are subject to unexpected shocks. For example, suppose that the automobile-buying public suddenly shift their allegiance from Ford to Toyota. This shift in demand toward Toyota and away from Ford has predictable effects on the stock price of each firm: Toyota's share price should increase and Ford's fall. Even though the expected returns are identical before the shock, they will not be afterward. And there is no reason to assume that Ford's stock price will recover. Just because Toyota's share price went up does not mean that it will pull Ford along with it.

If the stock price for Ford and Toyota can diverge, the combination of stock prices reflected in the major indexes traded on the exchanges listed above are not any more likely to be related. Because the indexes—and this is true for domestic indexes of different industries—represent the valuation of different firms, there really is no reason why they should move together. In fact, Dwyer and Hafer show that even if the *expected returns* of two stocks are perfectly correlated, their *prices* show no stable relationship over time.[8] This means that stock indexes appear to move in a common direction some of the time, while in other times they do not. The upshot is that the morning forecast of how the U.S. market will fare based on what happened in Tokyo probably has little predictive value.

This does not mean that stock prices never move together, just that they do not have to. To continue with the example, suppose that there is a general increase in the demand for automobiles in the United States. This would positively affect the stock price of Ford, a domestic producer, and Toyota, a Japanese firm. Even though the latter may be headquartered in Japan, it sells many cars in the United States and the rise of auto demand has a positive affect on its stock price. This common increase in auto demand shows up as an increase in the share prices for both firms. World events also can similarly affect individual share prices across exchanges. It also should be noted that increased globalization of business increases the links between international stock markets. As firms become more diverse geographically, economic events in countries where they sell their goods impact the company's stock price. Some event in another country can, therefore, have similar effects on stocks traded in different exchanges.

To see how related movements in the major indexes are, Figure 7.1 plots three major stock price indexes: The DJIA, the FTSE from the London Exchange, and the Nikkei 225 from the Tokyo Exchange. Because each index takes on a wide range of values, they are made comparable by indexing each to a value of 100 beginning in 1989.

Does Figure 7.1 suggest a predictable relation between these three indexes? From the figure one could argue that from 1989 through the next decade, the DJIA and the FTSE show quite similar behavior with both indexes increasing. That is not true, however, of the Nikkei. During this period the Japanese index was trending down. Indeed, this downward trend continues until the early 2000s when the Nikkei shows some slight upward movement. But contrast that with the DJIA and the FTSE. These indexes both show a drop beginning in 2000, but the magnitude of the decline and the length of the decline differ. This suggests that even though there are periods of apparent common movement, one cannot depend on such movements to occur over any given span of time. Thus, it is unlikely that stock prices, or stock indexes, are related in a predictable manner over time.

**FIGURE 7.1**
**Dow-Nikkei-FTSE and Adjusted Dow-Nikkei-FTSE, 1989–2005**

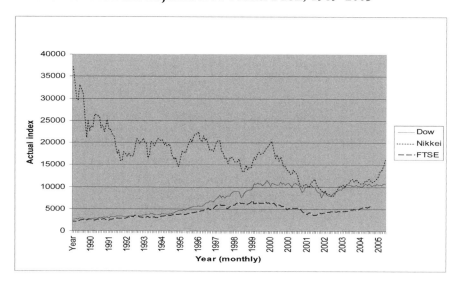

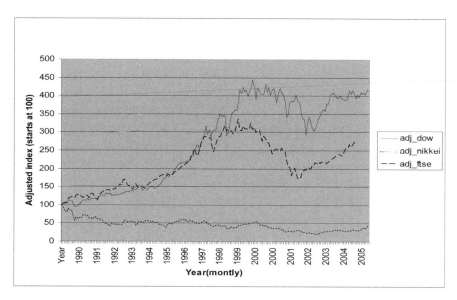

*Source*: www.wrenresearch.com.au/index.htm

## STOCK MARKETS AND ECONOMIC GROWTH

It would seem that having a stock exchange is a good thing for economic development. Indeed, looking at the number of individual stock exchanges around the world suggests that most feel it is better to have an exchange than not. Economists consider the issue of financial market development and economic growth to be one of the more important issues studied. Defining economic growth as the percentage increase in real per capita output (usually measured as real Gross Domestic Output [GDP]) over time, does financial market development—the introduction of a stock exchange—lead to greater economic growth?

In basic terms, stock markets help allocate financial capital between those individuals needing funds—firms—and those individuals with financial capital to lend—savers. When someone decides to buy a firm's stock, they are buying a claim to part of that firm's future earnings. Unlike bonds, which are a claim on the firm's assets, owning stock gives shareholders some right to future earnings. If the firm goes bankrupt, the stock becomes worthless and the initial investment is lost. On the other hand, if the firm does well, the dividends paid by the firm may increase, or more people may want to buy the stock and the original share price increases. For instance, a share of Wal-Mart or Google today is worth much more than it was when those firms first went public.

One role of a stock market is to allocate funds from individuals who want to save—in this case invest with an eye for capital appreciation—to those firms who need the money for further development. This latter notion is often times seen as the crucial link between the existence of a stock market and economic growth. If the market is not there to allocate the funds, then some firms, even the ones that may be the next Wal-Mart or Google, may not get the money needed to expand. If firms are not able to expand, economic activity is negatively impacted. Multiply this notion across many firms and it is easy to see why many believe that having a stock market is a necessary condition to increase economic growth.

One approach to examine the link between stock markets and economic growth is to see if economies that experience high rates of economic growth also are characterized as having well-developed banking systems and stock markets. The analysis by Levine and Zervos, for instance, uses a sample of nearly fifty countries to see if there is a direct relation between the development of a country's financial markets and faster economic growth.[9] Of course, it is crucial to determine whether this outcome stems from having a developed banking system, a stock market, or some combination of the two. Looking into this question, the analysis indicates that each plays an important and independent role in increasing economic growth. In other words, once other factors that might explain economic growth are controlled for (education, political environment and stability, openness to foreign trade, etc.), improved economic growth is positively related to having a stock exchange.

Figure 7.2, reprinted from the study by Baier, Dwyer, and Tamura, further illustrates the effect of opening a stock market on the economic growth for several countries.[10] In all cases, the comparison is made between economic growth before and after the exchange is opened. The three panels give this comparison from three different perspectives. The top panel simply compares economic growth in the country before and after the stock market opens. That is, is the average growth rate of real income higher after the stock exchange opens than before? The superimposed line indicates that the likely relation is positive: Opening a stock exchange is related to a higher economic growth rate. The middle panel uses as its base of comparison the growth rate in the rest of the world. Does opening a stock exchange increase a country's economic growth rate *relative to the rest of the world*? There too, the results indicate that opening a stock exchange leads to an increase in economic growth relative to the rest of the world's growth rate. Finally, the last panel compares the pre-exchange and post-exchange opening change in the growth rate of the economy with the change in the growth rate in the rest of the world. The outcome still is positive: opening a stock market increases economic growth rates by more than the increases experienced in the rest of the world. The bottom line is that opening an exchange has positive economic benefits.

Other studies corroborate the finding of a positive correlation between trading activity and economic growth. Extending the study by Levine and Zervos, Claessens, et al. find that economic success sometimes has unexpected consequences.[11] It may not, in fact, be in every country's advantage to expend the resources necessary to develop a local stock exchange. There is some evidence that as companies become more successful, their capital needs outgrow the local exchange and they delist their shares, moving to larger, more sophisticated financial markets. If such out-migration is large enough, firms remaining on the local exchange may find it increasingly difficult to raise funds. They also may find that decreased activity in the local market pushes their share prices down.

Such results actually are consistent with the history of exchanges. For example, consider the fact that most of the exchanges discussed earlier and in previous chapters have grown from regional exchanges to become national or global in scope. Firms that once listed only with a local exchange moved to the national market, such as the NYSE, as their financing needs grew. In the United States, several regional exchanges continue to operate. For example, the Boston Stock Exchange, founded in 1834, is the third-oldest operating

## FIGURE 7.2
### Economic Growth before and after an Exchange Is Opened

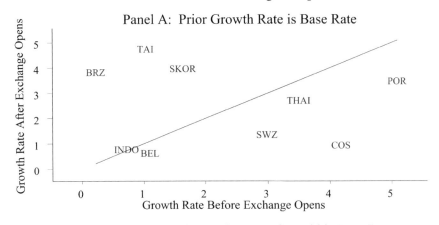

Panel A: Prior Growth Rate is Base Rate

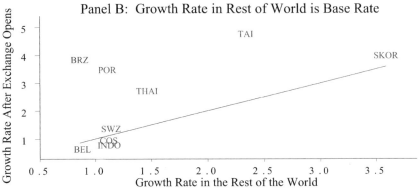

Panel B: Growth Rate in Rest of World is Base Rate

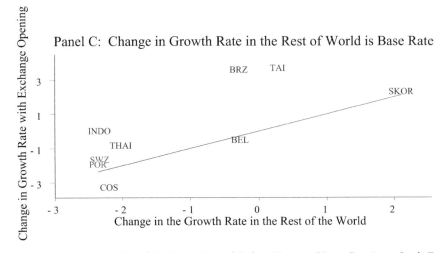

Panel C: Change in Growth Rate in the Rest of World is Base Rate

*Source*: Baier, Scott L., Gerald P. Dwyer, Jr. and Robert Tamura, "Does Opening a Stock Exchange Increase Economic Growth," *Journal of International Money and Finance* 23 (2004), 311–331. Figures are reprinted with permisson from Elsevier.

exchange in the United States. The Chicago Stock Exchange represents the merging of several smaller exchanges located in St. Louis, Cleveland, Minneapolis, and New Orleans. While the exchanges continue to operate, the national exchanges like the NYSE dominate trading activity.

One implication of this finding is that small countries may find it advantageous to forego the apparent benefits of opening a local stock exchange. Instead, it may be better to invest those resources to create an environment that facilitates the issuance and trading of shares abroad. Generally, this can be done by reducing domestic barriers to securities trading. Governments should attempt to improve corporate governance issues that may exist between the local and global markets. They also can alter accounting practices to be more universally acceptable and enforce securities rules in a manner consistent with other countries. If the natural outcome of economic and financial development is the migration of activity to the larger, more efficient markets, it may be more efficient to use the exchanges already in existence.

## SUMMARY

Stock exchanges do not open in an economic vacuum. It simply is not the case that stock markets open and economies then expand. Stock exchanges are formed to help allocate financial capital in an efficient manner. This is done through the trading of ownership rights in firms, whether through IPOs or through secondary trading. In all cases, stock markets provide very beneficial price signals to firms and investors of the expected success of different ventures. The long history of the major stock exchanges highlighted in this chapter is testament to the importance of these markets to the economic well-being of a country.

The fact that new exchanges are opened even today suggests that there probably is some economic gain from having an exchange compared to not having one. Indeed, the evidence from many studies indicates that opening a stock exchange has a positive effect on a country's growth. Even after accounting for other financial and societal developments, the presence of a stock market explains why some countries are economically better-off than others. Stock exchanges appear to be an indispensable component in the modern global economy.

## NOTES

1. This discussion is based on information from the official website of the Tokyo exchange, accessed at www.tse.or.jp. A source of additional information is Richard J. Teweles and Edward S. Bradley, *The Stock Market*, 5th ed. (New York: John Wiley, 1987).

2. Tokyo Exchange Fact Book, 2005.

3. This discussion is based on information from the stock exchange's official website. It can be accessed at www.londonstockexchange.com. Additional information was obtained from Teweles and Bradley (1987).

4. This discussion is based on information from Ron Yiu-wah Ho, Roger Strange, and Jenifer Piesse, "The Structural and Institutional Features of the Hong Kong Stock Market: Implications for Asset Pricing" (The Management Centre Research Papers, King's College, London, 2004).

5. This discussion is based on information taken from the official website of the Deutsche Borse Group. It can be accessed at http://deutsche-borse.com.

6. This discussion is based on information taken from the official website of the TSX Group. It can be accessed at www.tsx.com.

7. This discussion is based on material available at the official Euronext website. It can be accessed at www.euronext.com. Source: World Federation of Exchanges *Annual Report and Statistics* (2004).

8. Gerald P. Dwyer, Jr. and R.W. Hafer. "Are National Stock Markets Linked?" Federal Reserve Bank of St. Louis, *Review* (November/December 1988): 3–14.

9. Ross Levine and Sara Zervos, "Stock Markets, Banks and Economic Growth," *American Economic Review* 88, no. 3 (1998): 537–58.

10. Scott L. Baier, Gerald P. Dwyer, Jr., and Robert Tamura. "Does Opening a Stock Exchange Increase Economic Growth?" *Journal of International Money and Finance* (April 2004): 311–331.

11. Stijn Claessens, Daniel A. Klingebiel, and Sergio L. Schmulker. "The Future of Stock Exchanges in Emerging Economies: Evolution and Prospects" (Brookings-Wharton Papers on Financial Services, 2002), 167–202.

# Eight

## Summing It Up

By getting to this point you have covered quite of bit of territory. Believe it or not, the foregoing chapters only touched the surface of all there is to know about the stock market. Still, you should now be armed with enough information to understand what a stock price is and why it changes, what the different stock price indexes are, and on which exchanges, both domestic and foreign, they trade. Now, if one only had a copy of tomorrow's financial pages!

An important aspect of the stock market is that it is dynamic. The treatment of the market's development in Chapter Two reveals the hum of constant change. Not only is the stock market a business—the different exchanges compete for business just like shoe companies compete for your dollar—but it is a business on which the fortunes of many individuals and corporations depend.

The stock market promotes an efficient allocation of financial capital. Firms that are profitable and well managed see their stock prices rise while those firms losing money usually see their stock prices fall. These movements in stock prices reflect investors' preferences for how the two companies are managed or maybe what business they are in. So-called tech stocks did well in the 1990s because investors viewed them as the industry of the future. While this may be true, investor zeal in discovering the next Microsoft may have led some investors to lose site of the fundamentals upon which stock prices typically are based. Still, we have seen the stock market rally and fall back many times in its history. The good news is that its advances have always exceeded its declines. Today the stock market, measured by the Dow Jones Industrial Index (DJIA), is many times higher than it was just a decade ago. This translates into greater wealth for stockholders, of which most citizens can be counted. Indeed, more than ever before, more citizens have some stock ownership. While most of us may not directly own stock in any one firm, many have indirect ownership through mutual funds. Whether through our employer's retirement plan or through self-directed 401K plans, the financial well- being of an increasing number of U.S. households is related to events in the stock market. Perhaps that explains why a cable channel is dedicated to covering the stock market.

The ability of the market to allocate funds to their best use is one reason why most countries, big and small, advanced and emerging, have a stock exchange. The most cogent argument for this fact is the finding of scholarly studies that having a stock market usually is associated with improved economic growth. Even though it is difficult to disentangle the directional aspects of this relation—does having a stock market lead to better economic growth or does better growth give rise to the desire to trade stocks?—the evidence suggests that not having a stock market may slow economic advancement. This is not lost on many governments of countries that traditionally have not had market-oriented economies. For instance, the newly emerging economies of Eastern Europe and China all have opened stock exchanges. Although they pale in comparison to the activity of the U.S. market, they have not been active for two centuries either.

This allocative role of the stock market also shows up by the ever-increasing variety of financial instruments traded. Today, the market is linked to a much wider variety of instruments traded. For example, historically, the futures market dealt largely in agricultural goods, like corn and cattle, and raw materials such as copper and gold. That has changed. The futures market and the stock market are linked by contracts based on market indexes or even stocks in individual firms. This link increases the depth of the market and allows investors to spread risk. While some argued that this link was a major factor leading to the 1987 stock market crash, that notion has been dispelled by the performance since then.

The stock market is a major factor in any country's financial and economic health. This is why governments wish to prevent major catastrophes from occurring, like the crashes that we have covered. Following each major episode in the stock market, there arose some new set of government regulations. And while these regulations are meant to curtail some untoward behavior—from insider trading to outright manipulation and fraud—the stakes are so great that some see the potential gains as outweighing the possible costs. Government oversight and watchdog agencies, like the Securities and Exchange Commission (SEC) in the United States, exist to make financial markets and the transactions within as transparent as possible. Reducing the asymmetric information problem that arises between buyers and sellers—between investors and corporations, for example—is a key role for regulation.

What lies in store for the stock market of tomorrow? The current trend is toward increased electronic trading. Exchanges like the National Association of Securities Dealers Automated Quotation (NASDAQ) already perform without the face-to-face contact that has characterized other exchanges, most notably the New York Stock Exchange (NYSE). The day of the floor trader and the market specialist roaming the exchange's floor are numbered. It will not be long before the reporter covering the market will be seen in front of an electronic board of stock prices instead of being jostled by traders and runners closing deals.

There also is likely to be a further consolidation of exchanges, especially across national boundaries. This already has occurred in foreign markets. The Euronext exchange combines those of Brussels, Paris, and Amsterdam, among others. This type of consolidation raises the return to investors in the exchange and increases the depth of the market. Another example of such business-based activity occurred in early 2006. By May of 2006 the ownership of the London Stock Exchange became increasingly foreign. That is, the NASDAQ Stock Market (the company that owns the NASDAQ exchange) paid approximately $210 million to purchase 13.8 million shares of the London Stock Exchange (a publicly traded corporation). This raised NASDAQ's ownership in the London market to slightly over 24 percent. At the same time, the French insurance company AXA increased its ownership of the London Stock Exchange to slightly over 10 percent.

As with any corporation, ownership of stock gives the shareholder certain rights in the management of the company. In this case, both NASDAQ and AXA will be able to exert some influence on how the London Exchange is managed. Will such foreign ownership of a U.S. exchange occur? Before 2006, it would not have been possible for someone to own the NYSE. This is because the NYSE was owned by its members. However, the NYSE is now a publicly traded firm, just like General Electric or Boeing. This means that anyone owning a large enough block of the outstanding stock can have substantial influence over the operations of the exchange. Just as it happened with the London Stock Exchange, it is now possible that a foreign entity could purchase enough NYSE stock to own the exchange.

# Appendix: Companies Listed in the Dow Jones Industrial Average

## MAY 26, 1896

Beginning with this date, the Average was comprised solely of industrial stocks. Prior to this date, some of the stocks included railroads. The first published Average from the list of stocks was 40.94. Following its initial publication, the Average declined, reaching its lowest point in the history of the Average, 28.28 on August 8, 1896.

Chicago, Milwaukee & St. Paul
Chicago & North Western
Delaware & Hudson Canal
Delaware, Lackawanna & Western
Lake Shore Railroad
Louisville & Nashville

Missouri Pacific
New York Central
Northern Pacific pfd.
Pacific Mail Steamship
Union Pacific
Western Union

## AUGUST 31, 1925

American Can
American Car & Foundry
American Locomotive
American Smelting
American Sugar
American Telephone & Telegraph
American Tobacco
General Electric Company
General Motors Corporation
International Harvester

Kennecott
Mack Trucks
Sears Roebuck & Company
Texas Company
U.S. Realty
U.S. Rubber
U.S. Steel
Western Union
Westinghouse
Woolworth

## OCTOBER 1, 1928

On this date, the present version of the Dow Jones Industrial Average emerged. The list of stocks included in the Average was increased from twenty to thirty and several firms were substituted for others. Changes in the Average, in terms of the companies listed, would occur throughout its history.

Allied Chemical
American Can
American Smelting
American Sugar
American Tobacco B
Atlantic Refining
Bethlehem Steel
Chrysler
General Electric Company
General Motors Corporation
General Railway Signal
Goodrich
International Harvester
International Nickel
Mack Truck

Nash Motors
North American
Paramount Publix
Postum Incorporated
Radio Corporation
Sears Roebuck & Company
Standard Oil (N.J.)
Texas Company
Texas Gulf Sulphur
Union Carbide
U.S. Steel
Victor Talking Machine
Westinghouse Electric
Woolworth
Wright Aeronautical

## APRIL 21, 1976

This data is chosen to illustrate some of the changes that took place in the history of the Average. For example, companies listed in the Average today may not have appeared in the Average historically due to name changes. Some examples include the Nov 1, 1972 change from Standard Oil (N.J.) to Exxon; the May 30, 1973 change from Swift & Company to Esmark; or the April 21, 1976 change from International Nickel to Inco.

Allied Chemical
Aluminum Company of America
American Can
American Tel. & Tel.
American Tobacco B
Anaconda Copper
Bethlehem Steel
Chrysler
DuPont

Eastman Kodak Company
Esmark
Exxon Corporation
General Electric Company
General Foods
General Motors Corporation
Goodyear
Inco
International Harvester

International Paper Company
Johns-Manville
Owens-Illinois Glass
Procter & Gamble Company
Sears Roebuck & Company
Standard Oil of California

Texaco Incorporated
Union Carbide
United Technologies Corporation
U.S. Steel
Westinghouse Electric
Woolworth

## MAY 6, 1991

The companies included in the Average changes over time. On this date, the firms of Navistar International Corp., USX Corporation, and Primerica Corporation were replaced by Caterpillar Incorporated, Walt Disney Company, and J. P. Morgan & Company.

Allied-Signal Incorporated
Aluminum Company of America
American Express Company
American Tel. & Tel.
Bethlehem Steel
Boeing Company
Caterpillar Incorporated
Chevron
Coca-Cola Company
DuPont
Eastman Kodak Company
Exxon Corporation
General Electric Company
General Motors Corporation
Goodyear

International Business Machines
International Paper Company
J. P. Morgan & Company
McDonald's Corporation
Merck & Company, Inc.
Minnesota Mining & Mfg.
Philip Morris Companies Inc.
Procter & Gamble Company
Sears Roebuck & Company
Texaco Incorporated
Union Carbide
United Technologies Corporation
Walt Disney Company
Westinghouse Electric
Woolworth

## NOVEMBER 21, 2005

3M Company
Alcoa Incorporated
Altria Group Incorporated
American Express Company
American International Group
AT&T Incorporated
Boeing Corporation
Caterpillar Incorporated
Citigroup Incorporated
Coca-Cola Company

DuPont
Exxon Mobil Corporation
General Electric Company
General Motors Corporation
Hewlett-Packard Company
Home Depot Incorporated
Honeywell International Inc.
Intel Corporation
International Business Machines
Johnson & Johnson

J. P. Morgan Chase & Company
McDonald's Corporation
Merck & Company, Incorporated
Microsoft Corporation
Pfizer Incorporated

Procter & Gamble Company
United Technologies
Verizon Company
Wal-Mart Stores Incorporated
Walt Disney Company

Most recently, a change was made in the Average to reflect the fact that companies merge. The merger of AT&T with SBC Communications Inc. formed the new company AT&T Corporation, which replaces American Tel. & Tel in the list.

*Source*: Dow Jones Indexes, accessed at www.djindexes.com.

# Glossary

**American Depository Receipts (ADRs).** A relatively new addition to the financial markets; allow U.S. investors a simple means of investing in foreign stocks without going through the process of converting U.S. dollars into a foreign currency to buy the stock.

**At-the-money call option.** An option contract that has an exercise price that is identical to the current market price for the underlying instrument.

**Balanced fund.** A mutual fund that invests in both stocks and bonds.

**Bank run.** When depositors begin to withdraw funds based on fear that many banks are less likely to remit deposits.

**Bear markets.** Most stock prices are declining in value and stock returns are abnormally low and even negative.

**Bond fund.** A mutual fund that primarily invests in bonds.

**Bonds.** Securities that offer periodic payments in exchange for the firm receiving funds.

**Broker.** One who aids in buying and selling shares of stock by bringing two parties together to transact.

**Bull markets.** Stock returns on most stocks are yielding a higher return than their historical averages.

**Call options.** An option contract that allows the buyer of the option the right to buy something at a preagreed upon price and obligates the seller of the option to sell at this price.

**C Corporation.** A corporation that pays federal income taxes and generally has more than 100 shareholders; frequently listed on an exchange.

**Circuit breaker.** When trading is halted, based on chaotic trading conditions, until conditions are deemed appropriate for an orderly reopening of the market.

**Closed-end fund.** A mutual fund that issues a fixed number of shares to investors at the outset of the fund's operations.

**Closed-end fund discount.** When a closed-end fund sells in the market at a price below the fund's net asset value.

**Closed-end fund premium.** When a closed-end fund sells in the market at a price above the fund's net asset value.

**Common stock.** Stock that is not obligated to pay dividends.

**Contagion.** A situation in which the fear of loss spreads to other markets, generally widening overall losses.

**Corporate board of directors.** Voted in by stockholders; takes an active role in selecting the managers of the company who will oversee the day-to-day operations. The board is responsible for seeing that all shareholders' rights are recognized and maximized.

**Dealer.** One who aids in buying and selling shares of stock and will buy and sell stocks for their own portfolios as well.

**Diversification.** A situation in which losses are reduced by having offsetting gains, or at least smaller losses elsewhere.

**Diversification risk.** A risk that occurs from owning too few stocks, in which case one does not have gains in certain securities to offset losses in others.

**Dividends.** Payments from the corporation to the stock ownership. These can be in the form of cash or additional stock.

**Dynamic hedging/portfolio insurance.** The buying or selling of stocks or futures contacts to offset risk of price change to future price of stock.

**Earnings.** Generally a reference to the profits of the firm after all expenses and taxes have been paid.

**Efficient markets.** A characterization of the stock market in which all prices are said to immediately and fully reflect all available information.

**Equity fund.** A mutual fund that primarily invests in stocks.

**Exchange regulation.** A set of rules members must abide by, governed by an oversight body that can levy penalties for those who do not follow the rules; example Securities Exchange Commission (SEC) governing New York Stock Exchange (NYSE).

**Exchange-traded funds.** Single stocks that represent investments in a basket of other stocks or securities.

**Exercise price.** The preagreed upon for buying or selling an underlying security in an option contract.

**Federal Reserve Bank.** The nation's central bank, its goal: to serve as a source of liquidity to support the economic and financial system.

**401K Programs (403B, for public entities).** An optional retirement plan offered by many employers, which is tax advantaged, as investors do not pay taxes on gains until retirement.

**Fundamental market analysis.** Using data on a firm's profits and profit potential to assess the value of a given investment.

**Futures contracts.** Financial contracts that require the buyer to take delivery of the underlying commodity at a future date, while obligating the seller to make delivery. The price for future delivery is set today.

**Growth stock.** Stock in a corporation that generally pays low or no dividend and the price of each share is expected to increase over time.

**Hedge funds.** An investment (usually by wealthy people and firms) that buys a broad assortment of securities and other investment vehicles through various forms of global financial markets.

**Index mutual fund.** Invest in stocks that make up one of our stock indexes and generally have the lowest expense ratio of all stock mutual funds.

**Initial public offering (IPO).** Shares of stocks that are sold for the first time to the public.

**Insider selling/insider stock sales.** The purchase or sale of stock by someone intimately involved with the company based on information that the general public are not aware of. In many cases, this activity is illegal.

**In-the-money call option contract.** An option contract that has an exercise price below that would make it attractive to exercise an option today, ignoring the premium.

**Investment grade bond.** A bond highly rated by credit agencies and not likely to end up in default.

**Junk bond.** A bond rated as speculative, by credit rating agencies, with a high potential rate of return as well as a much higher probability of default.

**Large cap firms.** Corporations whose total value of shares outstanding (the product of the number of shares outstanding times the market value on one share) is deemed to be small, generally more than $5 billion in market capitalization.

**Leveraged buyout.** A purchase of a company by a small group of investors.

**Liquidity.** The ease of turning an asset into cash when selling it.

**Load fund.** A mutual fund has a load fee, which is a fee to invest, attached to it.

**Long position.** In an option contract the party buying an option contract is the party given the option to act. In a futures contract, the long position is the party accepting delivery in the future.

**Margin.** The actual dollar amount that must be provided (up front) by an investor taking a derivative position.

**Margin investing.** Buying stocks with borrowed money.

**Market capitalization.** Measured by taking the number of shares that a firm has outstanding and multiplying it by the share price.

**Market crash.** A situation in which the decline in stock prices is extreme, such as seen in October 1929 or October 1987.

**Mini stock index futures contracts.** Smaller notional value than stock index futures, generally have about one-fifth the notional value and margin compared with traditional stock index futures contracts.

**Mutual fund.** A financial intermediary that accepts money from investors and then turns around and buys a variety of securities. The intermediary decides on the investments made.

**No-load fund.** A mutual fund that does not charge an investor a fee upfront to invest.

**Notional value.** The total amount of stock that is deliverable in a stock derivative instrument.

**Open-ended mutual funds.** No fixed number of shares offered by the fund.

**Option premium.** The price of an option; also is the term used in the insurance industry to describe what a buyer of an insurance policy must pay.

**Options contract.** Obligates only one party to act, giving the other party the option to do something.

**Out-of-the-money option.** An option contract that has an exercise price that would be too expensive to exercise the option today.

**Over-the-counter.** Selling financial instruments through a means in which buyers and sellers do not necessarily meet together physically.

**Pension plans.** Plans that allow employees to save for retirement, many times employers match employee savings up to a limit.

**Preferred stock.** Stock that is obligated to pay dividends.

**Private stock/ private placement.** Stock in companies that are not publicly listed, generally having fewer than 500 shareholders.

**Publicly traded stock.** Stocks that are registered with the SEC.

**Put option.** An option contract that grants the buyer of the option the right to sell something at a preagreed upon price, and obligates the seller of the option to sell at that same price.

**Return.** The total compensation given to stockholders, which can be in the form of dividends or capital gains.

**Risk.** The possibility of financial loss (or gain).

**S Corporation.** A corporation that has no direct federal income tax liability, but passes this on to shareholders who pay taxes on earnings as individuals. Generally has less than 100 shareholders and is not listed on an exchange.

**Secondary market transaction.** Represents an exchange between two investors where the firm for which the stock represents an ownership obligation receives nothing from the transaction.

**Secondary offering.** Indicating that the stock has already been offered once before, representing another source of new funds for the corporation.

**Security.** A financial instrument that represents a contract of ownership and payment that is generally standardized to increase its liquidity.

**Securities Exchange Commission (SEC).** Regulates securities industry in the United States. Corporate Division oversees the disclosure of corporate information regarding financial conditions of firms with publicly traded stock.

**Share of stock.** Allows the shareholder a right to a pro rata share of the business's profits or, in the case of liquidation, the pro rata right to the value of the business's assets in excess of its liabilities

**Short position.** In the case of an option contract, this is the writer of the option, the seller of the option contract. In the case of a futures contract, this is the party obligated to make delivery. In the case of an individual stock, this is a party that sells a stock after borrowing it from another party, hoping the price will fall and they will be able to buy it back at a lower price.

**Single-stock futures contract.** A futures contract that calls for delivery of an individual stock instead of a basket of stocks that comprise some index.

**Small cap firms.** Corporations whose total value of shares outstanding (the product of the number of shares outstanding times the market value on one share) is deemed to be small, generally less than $1 billion in market capitalization.

**Stock.** Financial securities that represent ownership claims and are a contractual arrangement between two parties, the party investing in the firm and the firm. Financial asset to its owner; claim against the firm that issues it.

**Stock derivatives.** A financial contract that derives its value from a position related to the stock market or a particular stock.

**Stock (equity) fund.** A mutual fund that primarily invests in stocks.

**Stock exchange.** Physical location where traders (buyers and sellers) meet face-to-face to trade stocks.

**Stockholder.** A partial owner of the firm with limited liability, also someone who generally has right to vote in the election of the board of directors.

**Stock index.** A single measure of a basket of stock prices, for example: the basket of thirty stocks that underlie the DJIA.

**Stock index futures contracts.** A futures contract that calls for delivery of an index (basket) of stocks.

**Stock return.** The sum of all gains from investment divided by the amount originally invested.

**Systemic risk.** A risk that is systemwide and cannot be reduced by investing in a diversified basket of securities.

**Technical market analysis.** To predict a stock's future performance from its past behavior and its trading volume.

**Value stock.** Stock in a corporation that generally is selling at a low price, especially when benchmarked against the earnings of the company.

**Wealth.** The difference between the value of assets and liabilities at a point in time.

# Bibliography and Online Resources

## BOOKS

Arbel, Avner, and Albert E. Kaff. *Crash: Ten Days in October . . . Will It Strike Again?* New York: Longman Financial Services, 1989.

Brooks, John. *The Go-Go Years.* New York: Weybright and Talley, 1973.

Cooke, Gilbert W. *The Stock Markets.* Cambridge, MA: Schenkman, 1969.

Dwyer, Gerald P., Jr., and R.W. Hafer, eds. *The Stock Market: Bubbles, Volatility, and Chaos.* Boston: Kluwer, 1990.

Elias, David. *DOW 40,000: Strategies for Profiting from the Greatest Bull Market in History.* New York: McGraw-Hill, 1999.

Evans, Lawrance Lee, Jr. *Why the Bubble Burst: US Stock Market Performance since 1982.* Northampton, MA: Edward Elgar, 2003.

Federal Reserve Bank of Boston. *Panic of 1907.* Boston. n.d. Available at www.bos.frb.org.

Galbraith, John Kenneth. *The Great Crash: 1929.* Boston: Houghton Mifflin, 1955.

Kindleberger, Charles P. *Manias, Panics, and Crashes: A History of Financial Crises.* New York: Basic Books, 1978.

Lawerence, Joseph Stagg. *Wall Street and Washington.* Princeton, NJ: Princeton University Press, 1929.

Mahar, Maggie. *Bull: A History of the Boom, 1982–1999.* New York: HarperBusiness, 2003.

Medberry, James K. *Men and Mysteries of Wall Street.* Boston: Fields, Osgood, 1870.

Metz, Tim. *Black Monday: The Catastrophe of October 19, 1987 . . . and Beyond.* New York: William Morrow, 1988.

Saunders, Anthony, and Lawrence J. White, eds. *Technology and the Regulation of Financial Markets.* Lexington, MA: Lexington Books, 1986.

Shiller, Robert J. *Irrational Exuberance.* Princeton, NJ: Princeton University Press, 2000.

Siegel, Jeremy J. *Stocks for the Long Run: The Definitive Guide to Financial Market Returns and Long-Term Investment Strategies*, 3rd ed. New York: McGraw-Hill, 2002.

Sobel, Robert. *A History of the New York Stock Exchange, 1935–1975*. New York: Weybright and Talley, 1975

————. *The Big Board: A History of the New York Stock Market*. New York: Free Press, 1965.

————. *The Great Bull Market: Wall Street in the 1920s*. New York: WW Norton, 1968.

Teweles, Richard J., and Edward S. Bradley. *The Stock Market*, 5th ed. New York: John Wiley, 1987

Western, David L. *Booms, Bubbles and Busts in US Stock Markets*. London: Routledge, 2004.

Wigmore, Barry A. *The Crash and Its Aftermath: A History of Securities Markets in the United States, 1929–1933*. Westport, CT: Greenwood Press, 1985.

## ARTICLES

Allen, Franklin, and Richard Herring. "Banking Regulation versus Securities Market Regulation." The Wharton School Financial Institutions Center, Working paper 01–29 (2001).

Baier, Scott L., Gerald P. Dwyer, Jr., and Robert Tamura. "Does Opening a Stock Exchange Increase Economic Growth?" *Journal of International Money and Finance* (April 2004): 311–331.

Dwyer, Gerald P., Jr., and R.W. Hafer. "Are National Stock Markets Linked?" Federal Reserve Bank of St. Louis *Review* (November/December 1988): 3–14.

Claessens, Stijn, Daniel A. Klingebiel, and Sergio L. Schmulker. "The Future of Stock Exchanges in Emerging Economies: Evolution and Prospects." Brookings-Wharton Papers on Financial Services (2002): 167–202.

Greenspan, Alan. "The Challenge of Central Banking in a Democratic Society." Remarks delivered at the Annual Dinner and Francis Boyer Lecture of the American Enterprise Institute for Public Policy Research, Washington, D.C., December 5, 1996. Available at www.federalreserve.gov/boarddocs/speeches/1996.

Greenwald, Bruce, and Jeremy Stein. "The Task Force Report: The Reasoning behind the Recommendations." *Journal of Economic Perspectives* 2, no. 3 (Summer 1998): 3–23.

Haddock, David D. "The Swiftness of Divine Retribution and its Tendency to Mistake its Target: An Analysis of the Brady Report." In *The Stock Market: Bubbles, Volatility, and Chaos*, eds. Dwyer and Hafer, 179–195. Boston: Kluwer, 1990:.

Hall, Robert. "Struggling to Understand the Stock Market." *American Economic Review* 91, no. 2 (2001): 1–11.

Ho, Ron Yiu-wah, Roger Strange, and Jenifer Piesse. "The Structural and Institutional Features of the Hong Kong Stock Market: Implications for Asset Pricing." The Management Centre Research Papers, King's College, London 2004.

Jorgenson, Dale W. "Information Technology and the U.S. Economy." *American Economic Review* 91, no. 1 (2001): 1–32.

Levine, Ross, and Sara Zervos. "Stock Markets, Banks and Economic Growth." *American Economic Review* 88, no. 3 (1998): 537–558.

Macey, Johnathan R. "Regulation and Disaster: Some Observations in the Context of Systemic Risk." *Brookings-Wharton Papers on Financial Services* (1998).

Parry, Robert T. "The October '87 Crash Ten Years Later." Federal Reserve Bank of San Francisco *Economic Letter* 96–332 (1997).

## ONLINE RESOURCES

### US Stock Exchanges (Indexes)

American Stock Exchange (AMEX), http://www.amex.com.
Dow Jones Industrial Average (DJIA), http://www.djindexes.com/mdsidx.
National Association of Securities Dealers Automated Quotations (NASDAQ), http://www.nasdaq.com.
New York Stock Exchange (NYSE), http://www.nyse.com.
Russell Index, http://www.russell.com/us/indexes/us.
Wilshire Index, http://www.wilshire.com/Indexes.

### Related Exchanges

Chicago Board of Trade, http://www.cbot.com.
Chicago Mercantile Exchange, http://www.cme.com.

### International Stock Exchanges (Indexes)

Euronext (Euronext 100), http://www.euronext.com.
Frankfurt (DAX), http://deutsche-boerse.com.
Hong Kong (Hang Seng), http://www.hkex.com.hk.
London Stock Exchange (FTSE 100), http://www.londonstockexchange.com.
Tokyo Stock Exchange (Nikkei 225), http://www.tse.or.jp/english.
Toronto (TSE), http://www.tsx.com.

### Financial Press

*Barron's*, http://online.barrons.com.
*Bloomberg*, http://www.bloomberg.com.

The *Economist*, http://www.economist.com.
*Financial Times*, http://www.ft.com/home/us.
*Investor's Business Daily*, http://www.investors.com.
The *Wall Street Journal*, http://online.wsj.com.


## Financial Data

Hoover's, http://www.hoovers.com.
Moody's, http://www.moodys.com.
Standard & Poor's, http://www.standardandpoors.com.


## Government Agencies; Professional Organizations

Association of Investment Management and Research (CFA Institute), http://www.cfainstitute.org.
Federal Reserve System, http://www.federalreserveonline.org.
Financial Accounting Standards Board, http://www.fasb.org.
Futures Industry Association, http://www.futuresindustry.org.
International Swaps and Derivatives Association, http://www.isda.org.
National Association of Securities Dealers, http://www.nasd.com.
Public Company Accounting Oversight Board, http://www.pcaobus.org.
Securities and Exchange Commission, http://www.sec.gov.
Securities Industry Association, http://www.sia.com.


## General Information for Investors

Investorguide.com, http://www.investorguide.com.
Investorwords.com, http://www.investorwords.com.

# Index

## ABOUT THE AUTHORS

RIK W. HAFER is Professor and Chairman in the Department of Economics and Finance, and Director of the Office of Economic Education and Business Research, Southern Illinois University, Edwardsville. He served as Research Officer with the Federal Reserve Bank of St. Louis and his articles on monetary policy and financial markets have appeared in such publications as the *Wall Street Journal, International Economic Journal, Economic Review*, and the *Journal of Business*. He is the author or editor of several books, including *The Stock Market: Bubbles, Volatility, and Chaos, How Open Is the U.S. Economy?*, and *The Federal Reserve System* (Greenwood, 2005).

SCOTT E. HEIN is Briscoe Chair of Bank Management and Finance at Texas Tech University, where he teaches courses in the management of financial institutions, multinational financial management, money and capital markets, and the U.S. financial system. He also serves as Visiting Scholar at the Federal Reserve Bank of Atlanta and Chief Economist at Islay Opportunity Fund. He has published many articles in such publications as the *Journal of Financial Research, Applied Financial Economics*, and the *Journal of Banking and Finance*, and is on the board of editors for the *Quarterly Journal of Business and Economics*.